SOUTH-WEST ENGLAND AND WALES — 120

Blenheim Palace	122
Berkeley Castle	126
Harlech Castle	128
Caernarfon Castle	132
Beaumaris Castle	138

SCOTLAND — 140

Traquair House	142
Edinburgh Castle	146
The Palace of Holyroodhouse	152
Linlithgow Palace	162
Stirling Castle	166
Dunfermline Abbey and Palace	172
Scone Palace	174
Glamis Castle	176
Falkland Palace	182
Balmoral Castle	184
The Castle of Mey	188
Index	190
Credits	192

A Map of Royal Britain

Foreword

One of the best ways of tracing the ups and downs of British history is to visit the buildings where some of the events were played out. Each of them tells a particular story, from the many dark deeds that have stamped their shadowy mark on the Tower of London to the medieval stones of Scone Palace, which witnessed the coronations of a succession of Scottish kings.

It is difficult to resist the thrill of visiting places where huge national dramas have been played out, such as the room in the Palace of Holyroodhouse where Mary, Queen of Scots' secretary was murdered in front of her; the bedroom in Kensington Palace in which a young princess was woken to be told she had become Queen Victoria; or Edward I's 'iron ring' of castles that succeeded in subduing the Welsh lands he was trying to conquer. It is in such places that history shakes off its sometimes dusty image and comes dramatically alive.

All the buildings that appear in this book have been chosen because of their associations with British royalty. Some of them are obvious choices, such as Buckingham Palace, while others are less well known but still deserving of attention. They are all open to the public for at least part of each year, and they offer a fascinating insight into English, Scottish and Welsh royal history. Each entry is accompanied by the relevant travel information as well as the address of a website giving further details.

Some of the buildings in *Royal Britain* – including Royal Osborne and the Royal Pavilion – have been cherished homes in the past, even though they no longer perform that function today. Others, such as Sandringham House and Buckingham Palace, are still home to the current royal family. However, completely private residences, such as Highgrove House (the home of the Prince of Wales and the Duchess of Cornwall) and Gatcombe Park (the home of Princess Anne and Vice-Admiral Timothy Laurence), have not been included because they are not open to the public.

– Jane Struthers

Royal Britain map key

SOUTH-EAST ENGLAND AND EAST ANGLIA
① Sandringham House
② Hatfield Palace
③ Windsor Castle
④ Hampton Court Palace
⑤ Kew Palace [in inset box]
⑥ Hever Castle
⑦ Leeds Castle
⑧ The Royal Pavilion
⑨ Royal Osborne
⑩ Carisbrooke Castle

LONDON
⑪ Buckingham Palace
⑫ The Tower of London
⑬ Somerset House
⑭ Kensington Palace
⑮ St James's Palace
⑯ The Palace of Westminster
⑰ Eltham Palace
⑱ The Banqueting House
⑲ The Queen's House

SOUTH-WEST ENGLAND AND WALES
⑳ Blenheim Palace
㉑ Berkeley Castle
㉒ Harlech Castle
㉓ Caernarfon Castle
㉔ Beaumaris Castle

SCOTLAND
㉕ Traquair House
㉖ Edinburgh Castle
㉗ The Palace of Holyroodhouse
㉘ Linlithgow Palace
㉙ Stirling Castle
㉚ Dunfermline Abbey and Palace
㉛ Scone Palace
㉜ Glamis Castle
㉝ Falkland Palace
㉞ Balmoral Castle
㉟ The Castle of Mey

South-east England and East Anglia

After the Normans invaded England in 1066, the architectural landscape of the country changed forever. Castles sprang up like mushrooms with the purpose of subduing the newly conquered English and repelling other hopeful foreign invaders. Windsor Castle, which is now one of the best-known royal residences in the world, began life as a simple motte and bailey fort. Some of the buildings in this part of Britain were intended to be private homes to which members of royalty could retreat when necessary, and Sandringham House in Norfolk continues to fulfil this essential function.

▶ *Brighton's Royal Pavilion is steeped in history. The showcase of architects Henry Holland and John Nash, the building was breathtaking in its extravagance and decoration even in the lavish Regency era.*

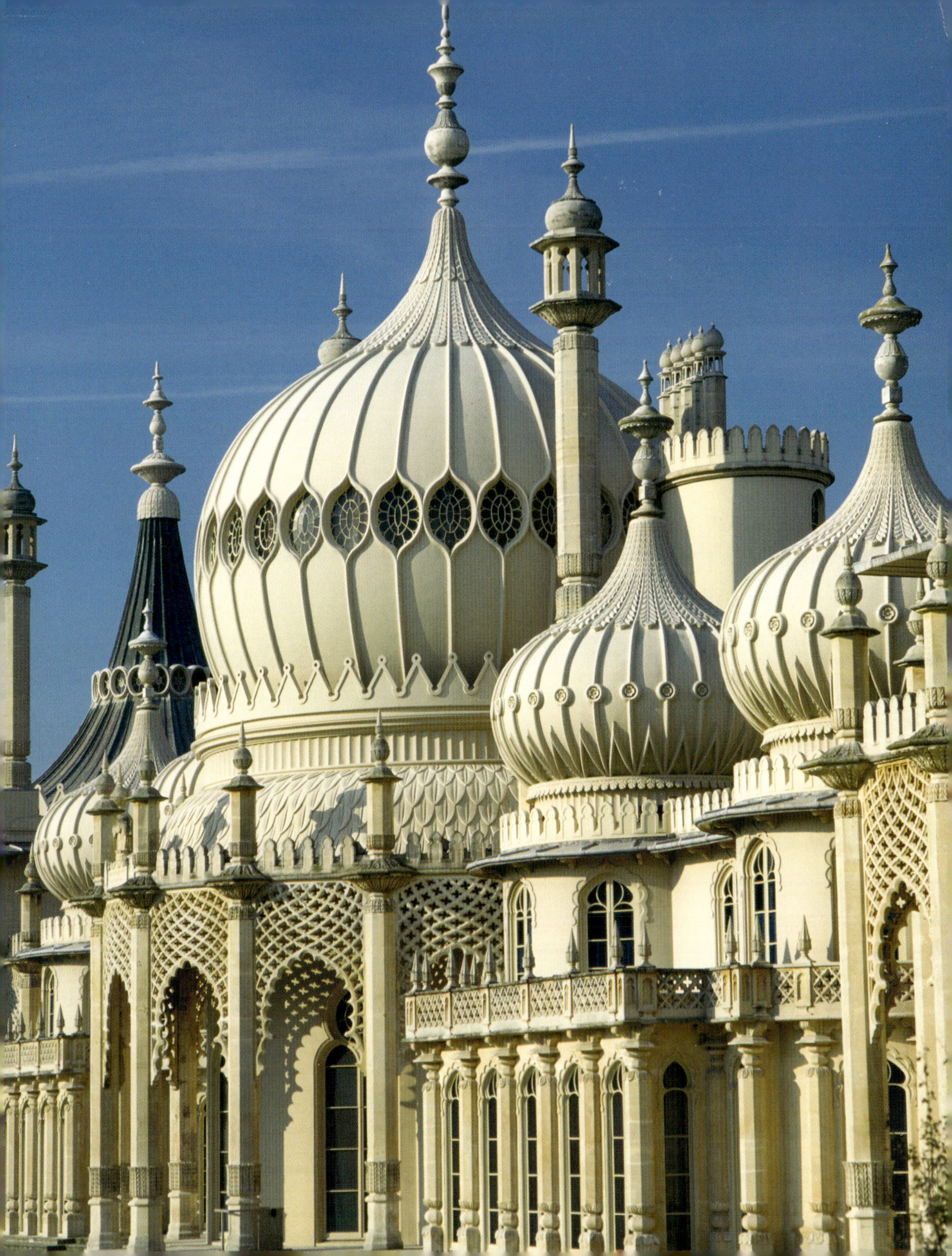

SANDRINGHAM HOUSE
Norfolk

KEY DATES

✠ *1862 Sandringham estate bought by the Prince of Wales*

✠ *1863 Marriage of Edward, Prince of Wales to Princess Alexandra of Denmark on 10 March*

✠ *1869–70 House enlarged*

✠ *1881–3 Ballroom added onto the house*

✠ *1891 Fourteen rooms and the roof are ruined by a serious fire in November*

✠ *1895 Prince Albert (later George VI) born at York Cottage on 14 December*

✠ *1932 First Christmas radio broadcast live from Sandringham by George V*

✠ *1936 Death of George V at Sandringham on 20 January*

✠ *1952 Death of George VI at Sandringham on 6 February*

✠ *1961 Lady Diana Spencer born at Park House on 1 July*

Sandringham House has always been more of a private home than a palace. Since the 1870s it has offered the royal family a private retreat from the heavy demands of state. For George V, it was 'the place I love better than anywhere else in the world'.

A family home

The Sandringham estate was acquired in 1862 by the Prince of Wales, later Edward VII, from the Hon. Charles Spencer Cowper. The Georgian house, while perfectly pleasant, was not nearly large enough for the prince's needs. After his marriage to the Danish Princess Alexandra in 1863, it was enlarged between 1869 and 1870 in the style of a comfortable country house. Sandringham was never intended to be a palace, so there was no need for any state function rooms. Besides, when foreign royalty came to stay, they were usually relatives of the prince or princess – Queen Victoria, whose children married into several foreign royal families, was known as 'the grandmother of Europe' – and their visits could be conducted in a very relaxed fashion. State visits were thus for London; family visits for Sandringham.

After a major fire in 1891, the house was extended once again and an east wing in red brick and brown carstone was built – a marked contrast to the red brick and yellow stone of the rest of the house.

▶ *The Small Drawing Room has an intimate atmosphere. The walls are hung with English silk and the seat covers of the Sheraton-style armchairs were stitched by Queen Mary in 1935.*

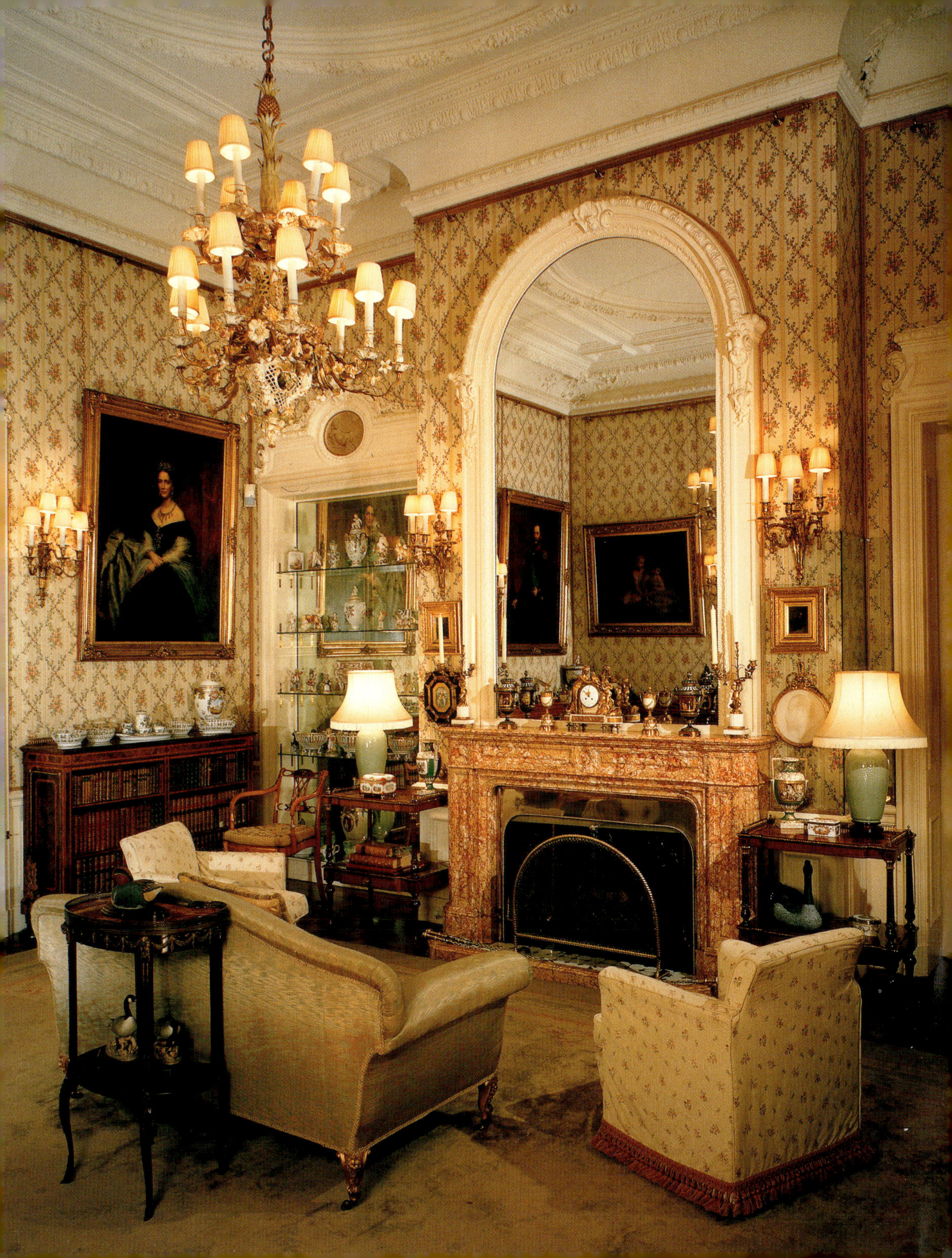

A social prince

At the time the Prince of Wales bought Sandringham he was in need of something to occupy his time and energy. His father, Prince Albert, had died unexpectedly the year before in 1861, and his mother, Queen Victoria, had immersed herself in widowhood and showed little sign of ever emerging from it. Nevertheless, she still kept a firm grip on her constitutional duties and was reluctant to let her eldest son help her in any way. Barred from any involvement with the official side of the monarchy, the Prince of Wales took over the social side instead. His mother had effectively disappeared from public view, leaving a huge gap that needed to be filled, and it was important to maintain a strong presence among the British people. Together, the newly married Prince and Princess of Wales embarked on the duties of constitutional monarchy: opening bridges, planting trees and meeting the people. They also became the pivot around which the highest echelons of fashionable Victorian society revolved.

A country retreat

The Prince and Princess of Wales had two homes: Sandringham in Norfolk and Marlborough House in Pall Mall, London. Although the Prince's life in London attracted a good deal of high-minded criticism and whispers of scandal (he was never short of mistresses), his visits to Sandringham received less censure.

> ### INTERESTING FEATURES
> - The Norwich Gates
> - The Saloon
> - The Small Drawing Room
> - The Drawing Room
> - The Ballroom
> - The museum

Here he could behave like a typical hunting-shooting-fishing member of the aristocracy, visiting his tenants, throwing country house parties for his many friends and generally setting a good example to the locals. After Queen Victoria's death on 22 January 1901, the royal couple became King Edward VII and Queen Alexandra, and Sandringham became an even more welcome retreat from the rigours of duty and protocol.

Edward VII and his cronies spent much time in the billiard room at Sandringham, where one can imagine them all smoking, drinking and exchanging risqué stories of female conquests. Queen Alexandra's province was the large, elegant Drawing Room, where she entertained a great deal. This room was also loved by her daughter-in-law, Queen Mary, who collected the jade and crystal that is on display there.

▶ *Princess Alexandra influenced the landscaping of the grounds. She preferred the new, naturalistic, unfussy style pioneered by William Robinson.*

George V

After Edward died on 6 May 1910, Sandringham passed to his only surviving son and heir, George V. Queen Alexandra still visited Sandringham, however, and died there on 20 November 1925.

George V and Queen Mary adored Sandringham, living in the modest York Cottage on the estate rather than in the 'big house', and all their children, with the exception of the Prince of Wales (later Edward VIII), were born on the estate. Harold Nicolson, the MP and diarist, wrote, 'There is nothing to differentiate the cottage from any of the villas at Surbiton… The King's and Queen's baths had lids that shut down so that when not in use they could be used as tables.'

Like his father, George V loved shooting at Sandringham, using cartridges stamped with a tiny red crown. Game birds were plentiful, which was just as well, as 10,000 of them were killed during one four-day shoot. He was also fond of big game hunting, and in 1928 he created a museum of trophies in rooms attached to the stable block.

▲ *The walled garden is one of the many small gardens found within the grounds of the Sandringham estate.*

George V died peacefully at Sandringham on 20 January 1936, a year that was to have momentous consequences for Britain, as it saw three kings sit on the throne: George V, Edward VIII and George VI.

The creation of a relaxed home

Edward VIII had little time or affection for Sandringham during his short reign. He also abominated one of the traditions of the house, introduced by his grandfather, Edward VII, of keeping the clocks half an hour fast (or 'Sandringham time') to have as much daylight as possible for shooting. Following his abdication from the throne, the newly styled Duke of Windsor sold Sandringham to his brother, the new George VI, who loved the place.

Public duties were arduous and nerve-racking for the new king, who was a shy man, but he took great solace from Sandringham. In the 1940s and 1950s, the estate felt like a very different place to the one on which George VI had grown up. The Countess of Airlie, lady-in-waiting to Queen Mary, wrote of George VI's tenure: 'There was no denying that the atmosphere of Sandringham was very much more friendly than in the old days, more like that of any home. One senses far more the setting of ordinary family life in this generation than in the last.'

George VI died at Sandringham on 6 February 1952 and his daughter became Queen Elizabeth II. Since then, the Queen and her family have spent each Christmas at Sandringham. They stay on until after the anniversary of George VI's death and the Queen's own ascension to the throne.

Modern connections

On 1 July 1961, Lady Diana Spencer was born at Park House on the Sandringham estate, where she grew up. In later life, she admitted that her roots were in Norfolk. Even before she married, Diana had royal connections: her grandfather, the 4th Lord Fermoy, leased Park House from George V, and her grandmother became a lady-in-waiting to the Queen Mother in 1955. Her father, Earl Spencer, was an equerry to George VI between 1950 and 1952 and subsequently worked in the household of Elizabeth II from 1952 to 1954. In 1981, Diana married Prince Charles; she was the first English bride of an heir to the British throne since 1659. Charles and Diana were divorced in 1996, and she was killed in a car crash in Paris on 31 August 1997.

Today, the Sandringham estate is a thriving commercial concern run by a land agent on the Queen's behalf. In addition to farming, the land is used for forestry, two stud farms and a 267-hectare (660-acre) country park open to the public. Yet, Sandringham still offers a safe haven to the royal family when they want to live a simpler life away from the public and media.

ⓘ information

Contact details

The Sandringham Estate
Estate Office
Sandringham
Norfolk
PE35 6EN

☎ +44 (0)1485 545408

The Sandringham estate
www.sandringhamestate.co.uk

Transport links

King's Lynn, 10 km (6 miles) and then the CoastHopper bus service

41 or Coastliner service from King's Lynn Bus Station

10 km (6 miles) north-east of King's Lynn

SANDRINGHAM HOUSE

HATFIELD PALACE
Hertfordshire

Hatfield Palace was built in 1480 for Cardinal Morton, Bishop of Ely and later Archbishop of Canterbury. In 1533 it fell into the rapacious hands of Henry VIII who wanted it for his daughters, Mary and Elizabeth (the future Mary I and Elizabeth I of England). Following a difficult childhood, much of which was spent at Hatfield, Elizabeth I had little interest in the palace. She preferred the nearby Theobalds House owned by her chief minister, William Cecil, later Lord Burghley. Her successor, James I of England and VI of Scotland, also preferred Theobalds House. James suggested to Lord Burghley's son, Robert Cecil, that they exchange properties, which they did in 1607.

Under an oak tree

In 1558, history was made at Hatfield Palace. Late in the morning of 17 November, the then Princess Elizabeth sat under an oak tree reading a book, unaware that her half-sister, Mary I, had died earlier that morning and that she was now queen. Elizabeth had already had vivid experiences of the dramatic twists and turns of fate. At the age of two, Henry VIII had denounced her as a bastard with no right to the throne and he had Anne Boleyn, his second wife and Elizabeth's mother, beheaded. Henry later changed his mind and declared Elizabeth third in line to the throne after her half-siblings, Edward and Mary, although he failed to declare her legitimate.

▶ *The Elizabethan knot garden in front of the Great Hall was painstakingly restored in the 1980s.*

KEY DATES

✣ **1480** Hatfield Palace is built for Cardinal Morton

✣ **1533** Birth of Princess Elizabeth (later Elizabeth I) on 7 September

✣ **1533** The palace is acquired by Henry VIII for his daughters

✣ **1558** Elizabeth I is told of her succession to the throne at Hatfield Palace on 17 November

✣ **1558** Elizabeth's first Privy Council held in the Banqueting Hall at Hatfield Palace on 20 November

✣ **1603** Death of Elizabeth I on 24 March

✣ **1607** James I of England and VI of Scotland exchanges Hatfield Palace for Lord Burghley's Theobalds House

✣ **1611** Construction of Hatfield House begins

✣ **1984** Restoration of the Elizabethan knot garden is completed

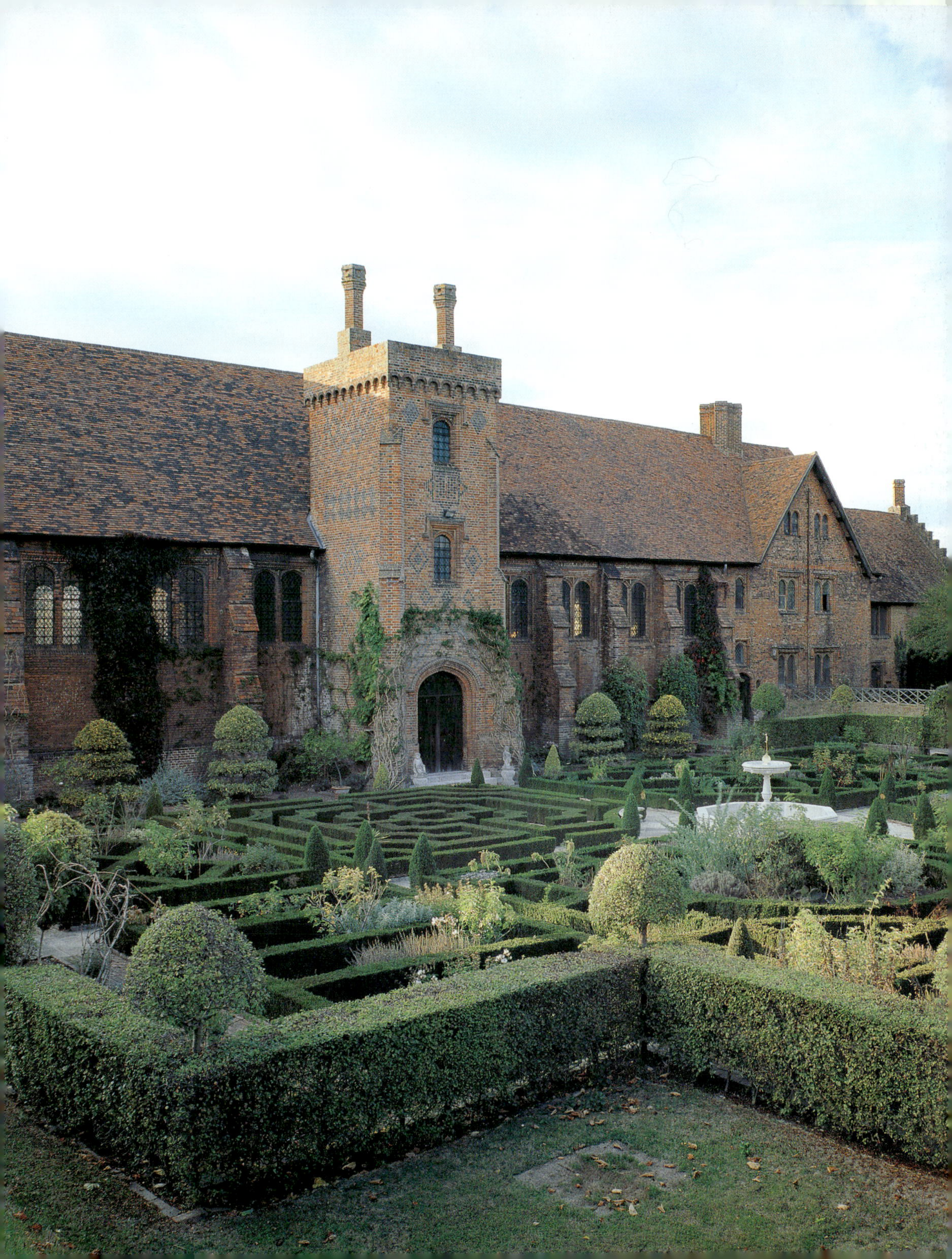

▲ *Hatfield Palace was Princess Elizabeth's home for part of her childhood. She lived an isolated existence before ascending the English throne as Elizabeth I.*

INTERESTING FEATURES

✠ The Marble Hall
✠ King James's Drawing Room
✠ The Banqueting Hall
✠ The Elizabethan knot garden

Hatfield House

Robert Cecil, now Earl of Salisbury and the new owner of Hatfield, wanted a house that reflected his importance. He ignored the existing royal palace and built a new house in an 'H' shape further up the hill. He hoped that James and his wife, Anne of Denmark, would visit frequently, and created a house that was fit for royalty.

The exterior domes and turrets were decorated with gold leaf and there were staterooms for important ceremonial occasions. One wing of the original Hatfield Palace still stands, having undergone extensive restoration in the 20th century. The Tudor Banqueting Hall in the palace is where Elizabeth I held her first Privy Council on 20 November 1558.

Hatfield House enjoyed its apotheosis during the Victorian and Edwardian eras when the 3rd Marquess (and 9th Earl) of Salisbury, Robert Gascoyne-Cecil, was prime minister. During that time the House became one of the most important and popular country houses in Britain and was once more a thriving hub of political and social activity.

information

Contact details

Hatfield House
Hatfield, Hertfordshire
AL9 5NQ

Hatfield House
www.hatfield-house.co.uk

+44 (0)1707 287010

Transport links

Hatfield station

Luton, Stansted and Heathrow

34 km (21 miles) from Central London; 11 km (7 miles) north of the M25 (junction 23) and 3 km (2 miles) east of the A1(M) (junction 4)

HATFIELD PALACE

WINDSOR CASTLE
Berkshire

KEY DATES

✠ *c.1100* Henry I has domestic lodgings in the castle

✠ *1165–71* New apartments built

✠ *1247–9* Gislebertus doors created for the king's chapel

✠ *1350* Work on the lower ward by Edward III begins

✠ *1357* Work on the upper ward by Edward III begins

✠ *1359* The Norman gateway built by Edward III

✠ *1675–8* Charles II creates new state apartments

✠ *1790 and 1792* Estates at Frogmore purchased

✠ *1969* Dedication of the King George VI Memorial Chapel on 31 March

✠ *1992* Fire breaks out at the castle on 20 November

✠ *1997* Restoration completed on 20 November

Windsor Castle enjoys several distinctions: it is the oldest occupied palace in Europe; the largest occupied castle in the world; and the Round Tower makes it one of the most easily recognized buildings worldwide. The castle can be seen for miles, thanks to its strategic position atop a chalk ridge above the River Thames west of London.

Establishing a motte and bailey castle

After William the Conqueror successfully invaded England in 1066, he built a series of castles encircling London, including at Windsor, to keep an iron grip on his new subjects and repel other would-be invaders. The area around Windsor was already familiar to English kings as they hunted deer there, thus by the time Henry II was on the throne, in the 12th century, it made sense to build a royal palace at Windsor. Henry built official rooms in the lower ward and a set of private rooms in the upper ward. He also replaced the original timber keep on top of the motte with one made of stone. This was the basis of what is now the Round Tower.

The Order of the Garter

Although successive kings made their mark on Windsor Castle, none had as big an impact as Edward III, who was born there in 1312. He financed work on Windsor from his successful wars in France, turning it into a fortified palace in which he spent much time. Edward

▶ Windsor Castle, the official residence of Her Majesty the Queen, has had an eventful history spanning 1,000 years.

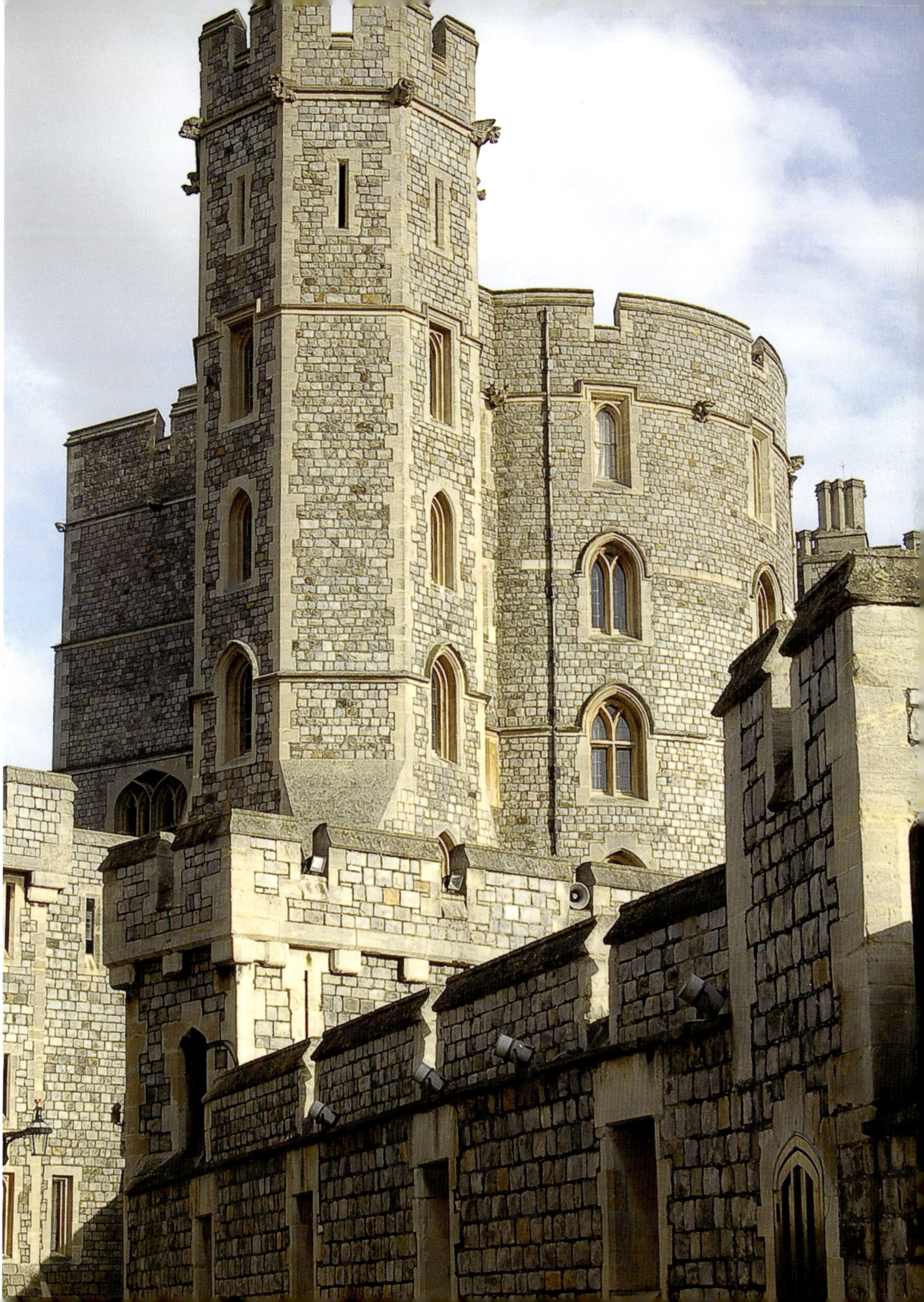

The kitchens at Windsor Castle are in the upper ward and were built during the reign of Edward III in the 14th century. The original timber roof has survived for six centuries.

was also responsible for founding the Order of the Garter, which was based on the medieval ideals of chivalry. This, the oldest chivalric order in Britain, is still bestowed as a mark of royal favour. The first ceremony of the Garter was held on 23 April 1348 on the festival of St George, the patron saint of England and also of soldiers. The existing King's Chapel was also renamed St George's Chapel. The Order's insignia are a garter and badge showing George and the dragon he slew.

St George's Chapel

In 1475, Edward IV commissioned Henry Janyns to redesign St George's Chapel in the Perpendicular Gothic style. Edward wanted his own funeral monument in the new chapel, although it was nowhere near ready when he died in April 1483. This was the era of the Wars of the Roses, fought between the Lancastrian and Yorkist royal houses; the Lancastrian king, Henry VI, had been murdered in 1471, probably on the orders of the Yorkist Edward IV. Henry's body was moved from Chertsey Abbey

INTERESTING FEATURES

- The Norman gateway
- The new ceiling of St George's Hall
- St George's Chapel
- The Royal Mausoleum at Frogmore
- Queen Mary's dolls' house
- The Drawings Gallery
- The Crimson Drawing Room
- The Great Kitchen
- The Jubilee Garden
- The Queen's Audience Chamber

in Surrey to St George's Chapel in 1485 and almost immediately miracles happened. This resulted in a cult centring around Henry's tomb. It also became a site of pilgrimage.

Henry VII noted this when, in 1493, he began to consider where he should be buried. He embarked upon an ambitious building project, pulling down part of St George's Chapel and erecting a Lady Chapel in its place. Work went well until 1498 when a lawsuit determined that Henry VI had actually wanted to be buried in Westminster Abbey and that his body should be transferred there. A Lady Chapel was duly built for him in the Abbey, although his body was never moved from Windsor.

Many succeeding monarchs have played their part in the evolution of St George's Chapel, which today is a rich and complex building that bears more resemblance to a cathedral than a chapel. It is lavishly decorated with oak carving, as befits a royal chapel, and was one of the most important in medieval Europe. There have been many royal weddings there, including that of the Prince of Wales (later Edward VII) to Princess Alexandra on 10 March 1863, and Prince Edward to Sophie Rhys-Jones on 19 June 1999. St George's is also the burial place of 10 sovereigns: Edward IV and Henry VI lie on either side of the high altar and the bodies of George III, George IV and William IV are in the royal vault. The body of Charles I was buried under the choir in a vault that already contained the coffins of Jane Seymour and Henry VIII.

St George's Chapel suffered badly during the Civil War, when many of its ornaments were removed and all the plate was melted down. The castle itself, in common with many other royal residences, was taken over by Parliamentarian forces and the rooms in the Upper Ward were turned into prisons for Royalists. When Charles II regained the throne in 1660, he had much work to do in restoring those residences damaged and sacked by the Parliamentarians.

Charles II

Charles wanted a baroque palace whose architecture reflected the importance of the Order of the Garter, so the buildings in the upper ward were remodelled at a cost of over £130,000. The new state apartments were created in 1675–8, after which work began on the royal chapel and St George's Hall. Antonio Verrio created the painted decorations, which established his career in Britain and led to many other prestigious commissions. Grinling Gibbons also established himself as a woodcarver of genius through his work at Windsor. Charles was responsible for buying back parcels of land within Windsor Great Park that had been sold off during the Civil War, and for planting the Long Walk of elms between 1683–5. His successors, William III and Queen Anne, contributed to the gardens, but the first two Hanoverian kings, George I and George II, had little interest in the castle and turned much of the upper ward into grace-and-favour apartments.

George III

Hampton Court conjured up unhappy family memories for George III, so he chose Windsor Castle as his main country residence. Rebuilding started in 1778, supervised by Sir William Chambers, who told the king that the castle could never be made into a comfortable home. Indeed, at the time, some of the state apartments were opened regularly to the public, and school children even played within the precincts of the castle.

In June 1790, a small house at Frogmore, to the south of Home Park, was purchased for George's consort, Queen Charlotte. This was followed, two years later, by the acquisition of the estate at Great Frogmore, and Charlotte enlarged and improved Frogmore House. The estate at Frogmore was formally linked to Windsor Castle in 1841, long after Charlotte's death, and became an official royal residence. That same year, Queen Victoria's mother, the Duchess of Kent, moved to Frogmore to live until her death on 16 March 1861.

The architect James Wyatt remodelled Frogmore House so successfully that he was appointed a surveyor-general in 1796 and commissioned to work on Windsor Castle. The work began in 1800 and was still unfinished in 1811 when George III became incapacitated by his condition, porphyria, a disorder of the blood that poisons the nervous system and brain – although he had been misdiagnosed as insane. He was pushed to the limit by grief at the death of his youngest daughter Amelia in 1811, and spent the rest of his life in an isolated set of rooms at Windsor Castle, lonely and blind,

▶ *St George's Hall, opposite, has the largest hammerbeam roof to have been created since the Middle Ages.*

24 SOUTH-EAST ENGLAND AND EAST ANGLIA

WINDSOR CASTLE 25

with the Star of the Order of the Garter pinned to his chest as a nostalgic reminder that he had once been king.

Expensive refurbishments

George III's son became Prince Regent, which added fuel to his burning desire to create exquisitely palatial royal residences. After being crowned George IV in 1820, he transformed St James's Palace, Buckingham Palace and Windsor Castle into magnificent palaces. In 1823, he moved into Windsor Castle but, as happened so often with him, found that it could not meet his needs. Parliament pledged £150,000 for the remodelling work, although it eventually cost close to £1 million. The Round Tower was raised by 9 metres (30 feet), the Long Walk was extended up to the castle and the George IV Gateway was created as the new main entrance. King George IV's Tower and the Cornwall Tower were built, and the exteriors of the buildings in the Upper Ward were given a Gothic look. George IV did not care for his father's apartments in the north range of the Upper Ward and opted instead for the east and south ranges, where a new set of rooms was built for him using a Gothic style for the processional and eating areas and a French style for the drawing rooms and royal apartments.

◀ *Windsor Castle has been occupied continuously for more than 900 years. After centuries of alterations, it now contains around 1,000 rooms.*

and cool temperatures in the rooms. She expected her guests to do the same. After the queen retired to bed each evening, the men were free to smoke in the billiard room at the end of the north wing, but this was so far from the rest of the castle that some guests were unable to find their way back to their rooms through the gloomy corridors – particularly since Victoria disliked gaslight, so the castle was lit by candles.

Windsor had particular significance for Victoria because her adored husband, Prince Albert, died there on 14 December 1861. For the rest of her life she kept his bedroom, the Blue Room, exactly as he had left it. Victoria created another shrine for Albert in the Albert Memorial Chapel, which was built in the shell of the old Lady Chapel in St George's Chapel. She also created the royal mausoleum at Frogmore, where she was buried beside her beloved Albert in 1901.

Victoria

Queen Victoria adored Windsor Castle, and it became the stage set for many state visits and family gatherings. However, visits to the castle could be a trial for those who felt the cold, as Victoria enjoyed plenty of fresh air

ⓘ information

Contact details

Windsor Castle
Windsor
Berkshire
SL4 1NJ

☎ +44 (0)20 7766 7304

The Royal Borough of Windsor and Maidenhead
www.windsor.gov.uk/site/things-to-do/windsor-castle-p43983

Transport links

Windsor

Green Line operates daily from Victoria Coach Station, London

M4 to exit 6; M3 to exit 6

WINDSOR CASTLE

HAMPTON COURT PALACE
Surrey

KEY DATES

✠ 1236 The Knights Hospitallers of St John of Jerusalem acquire the manor of Hampton

✠ 1514 Sir Thomas Wolsey leases the property

✠ 1537 Birth of the future Edward VI, Henry VIII's only surviving son, on 12 October

✠ 1654 Oliver Cromwell moves into the palace

✠ 1689 William III and Mary II move into the palace and embark on major building work

✠ 1838 Hampton Court opened to the public; by 1897 over 11 million people had visited the palace

✠ 1986 Hampton Court seriously damaged by fire

✠ 1992 Restored apartments opened by the Queen on 8 July

The early history of Hampton Court Palace is a moral tale that warns against the perils of greed, hubris and of reaching an exalted position that attracts envy. Although it is now one of the great royal palaces in Britain, if not the world, Hampton Court was originally the home of a commoner, Thomas Wolsey, whose star shone very brightly in the Tudor firmament before it was snuffed out by a situation he was powerless to control.

Thomas Wolsey

Born in the early 1470s, Wolsey was the son of an Ipswich butcher, but his ambition soon took him into the Church, where he climbed the ecclesiastical ladder in record time. Having been chaplain to Henry VII, he was in a good position when Henry's son, Henry VIII, succeeded to the throne in 1509. Wolsey quickly attained a series of bishoprics, which offered him great financial rewards as well as considerable prestige. After becoming Lord Chancellor and Cardinal in 1515, he immediately set about creating a home that would reflect his tremendous importance and wealth.

Wolsey had acquired the lease on Hampton Court in 1514 when it was still a relatively modest country house. It was not long before the place became a hub of activity, swarming with builders, carpenters and masons. Wolsey wanted a home in which he could

▶ *The astronomical clock in Clock Court was made in 1540 for Henry VIII by Nicholas Oursian. In Wolsey's day, Clock Court formed the inner courtyard of his home.*

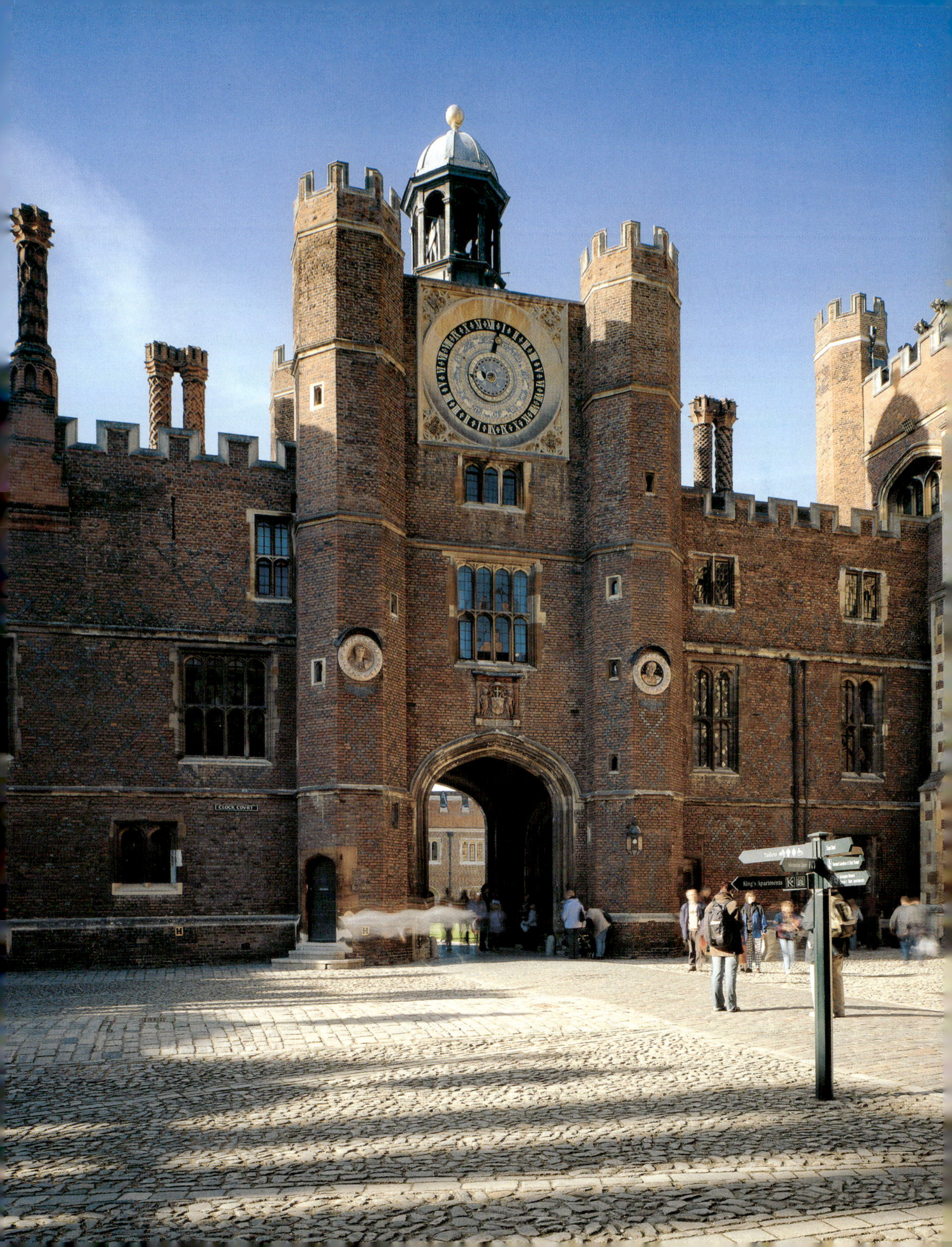
CLOCK COVRT
Toilets
King's Apartments

INTERESTING FEATURES

- The astronomical clock in Clock Court
- The gilded ceiling and royal pew in the Chapel Royal
- The Great Hall
- The Tudor kitchens
- The Renaissance picture gallery
- The King's Staircase
- The Queen's Dressing Room and bathroom
- The Great Maze
- The Painted Room in the Banqueting House
- The Privy Garden

entertain on a lavish scale, with a suite of apartments suitable for Henry VIII, his wife Catherine of Aragon and their daughter Princess Mary. Forty of Wolsey's guest suites were built around Base Court and each one offered an outer and an inner room, plus a lavatory (known at the time as a garderobe). The royal apartments were in what is now part of the Georgian rooms.

There was no doubt that Wolsey was in the ascendant as one of the most powerful men in the kingdom. However, his nemesis arrived in the guise of Anne Boleyn and the king's 'great matter'. Catherine had failed to produce a living male heir to the throne, a source of great concern. Henry needed to find a solution and he did not have to look far. He was obsessed with Anne Boleyn, one of Catherine's ladies-in-waiting, whose beauty, youth and apparent fertility were in marked contrast to the now faded charms of his wife. It became obvious to him that he must divorce Catherine and marry Anne, and it fell to Wolsey to arrange this with the Pope. The Pope refused to countenance such a step, and the problem was compounded by difficulties within Europe and the enmity Anne felt towards Wolsey. He had also become too powerful and rich for Henry's liking: Wolsey's wealth amounted to one-third of the ordinary revenues of the Crown. After further delays, over which he had no control, Wolsey's fate was sealed. He was arrested in October 1529, then pardoned, but was arrested again the following year and died on his way to the Tower of London.

Henry VIII

Hampton Court changed hands when Henry forced Wolsey to surrender it in 1528. This was, after all, a period in history when monarchs had absolute power, and Henry had much working in his favour. He was still a relatively young man with good cause to be optimistic when he took over the ownership of Hampton Court and so he embarked on a fresh round of building work. He also had plenty of money as his exchequer had been greatly increased by the spoils from the dissolution of the monasteries in 1536, which followed England's rebuttal of Catholicism and the beginning of the English Reformation. Hampton Court became a splendid royal palace with running water (the height of innovative luxury at the time), formal gardens, massive kitchens that can still be seen today, a magnificent Chapel Royal (Henry prided himself on his devout nature, although history views his character in a less sanctified light) and luxurious state and private apartments that were remodelled again and again according to his whims.

The Elizabethan court

Henry owned more than 60 houses and considered Hampton Court to be his fourth favourite after Whitehall Palace, Greenwich Palace and Windsor Castle. There was great joy at Hampton Court when Henry's only surviving and legitimate male heir, Prince Edward (later Edward VI), was born on 12 October 1537, followed by grief when his wife, Jane Seymour, died 12 days later; and optimism when he married his sixth wife, Catherine Parr, in the Holyday Closet above the Chapel Royal on 12 July 1543. After his death in 1547, Henry's Tudor heirs continued to visit Hampton Court but never carried out much building work. Elizabeth I almost died of smallpox at Hampton Court in 1562, which made her reluctant to go near it for some time, but eventually the Elizabethan court would celebrate Easter, Whitsun and some Christmases there. Plays were staged with elaborate preparation in the Great Hall, even to the extent of providing artificial snow. Nevertheless, Elizabeth thought the palace unhealthy and used it mainly to impress visiting dignitaries at important occasions. She was intolerant of certain smells, including those from the privy kitchen beneath her apartments, and the offending kitchen was moved to another part of the palace in 1567. The gardens pleased her, however, and she enjoyed working in them. When potatoes and tobacco plants were discovered in the New World, they were imported and planted at Hampton Court.

The Civil War

After Elizabeth died on 24 March 1603, her successor, James I (James VI of Scotland) enjoyed hunting in the park, and his son, Charles I, spent his honeymoon there in the summer of 1625 with his French bride, Henrietta Maria. Later on in his reign, Charles had less happy memories of the place, as he was imprisoned there in 1647, during the Civil War. It was at this point

32 SOUTH-EAST ENGLAND AND EAST ANGLIA

The King's Privy Chamber was the most important ceremonial room. William III sat under the throne canopy for his audiences with members of court.

that Hampton Court fell into the possession of parliamentary forces, who systematically stripped it of most of its treasures and sold them. The palace itself was sold to an Edmund Backwall in 1652, but was bought back for Oliver Cromwell after he became Lord Protector in 1653.

After the restoration of the monarchy in 1660, Hampton Court once again became a royal palace, although it was never a favourite of Charles II. It was, however, the perfect place for him to store important paintings during the Great Fire of London in 1666. During this time Charles II was also busily retrieving lost royal treasures: Oliver Cromwell's widow surrendered as many as 17 cartloads of royal belongings.

A second renaissance

Hampton Court enjoyed a second renaissance when William III and Mary II succeeded to the throne in 1689. The new king and queen liked both the palace and its grounds (and clean air for the asthmatic William), but they found the buildings antiquated and uncomfortable. As a result, Sir Christopher Wren was asked to pull down almost the entire Tudor palace, with the exception of the Great Hall, and to rebuild it in a modern style reminiscent of the magnificent Palace of Versailles. Despite allocating vast sums to the rebuilding work, William and Mary's budget failed to run to such drastic structural changes and they had to compromise: the old Tudor lodgings on the south and east sides of the palace were demolished and replaced with the royal couple's new apartments. William and Mary were impatient owners and wanted instant results, which translated into rushed and poor building work. This had tragic results in December 1689 when, only seven months after work had started, a large section of the south range collapsed, killing two workmen and injuring 11 others. There was a further setback in December 1694 when Mary died of smallpox, and building work was suspended until 1698. When work finally resumed, it was conducted by Wren's deputy, as Wren himself had submitted an estimate that was considered to be too expensive; the Nine Years War against France had just ended and the budget was tight. Sadly, William had little time to enjoy his palace, as he died in 1702 after breaking his collarbone when he fell from his horse while riding near Hampton Court.

Refurbishment of the Chapel Royal

Queen Anne inherited the throne and, with it, Hampton Court. However, the Queen's Apartments were still being built, so she had to stay in the King's Apartments. She enjoyed hunting, but her frail health meant she had to follow the hounds in a cart along a specially constructed track.

One of her greatest legacies was the refurbishment of the Chapel Royal, executed by Sir Christopher Wren. All that remains of the Tudor chapel is the intricate gilded ceiling installed by Henry VIII in 1535–6. The royal pew, which looks down on the chapel from the gallery above, was constructed for Queen Anne, necessitating rudimentary divisions across the beautiful old ceiling. Architectural vandalism is nothing new: unsympathetic changes to ancient buildings have been carried out down the centuries, sometimes by the most celebrated names.

The Hanoverian dynasty
When George I came to Britain from Hanover after attaining the throne in 1714, he could not speak English and preferred to stay out of the limelight. However, his son and daughter-in-law, the Prince and Princess of Wales (later George II and Queen Caroline), enjoyed court life and spent a great deal of time at Hampton Court. They used the Queen's Apartments from the summer of 1716 onwards.

During the Hanoverian dynasty there was invariably trouble between father and eldest son. George was jealous of his son's success and popularity, and finally banned the prince from court in 1717. George I held a full court at Hampton Court in 1718 before patching up the argument with his son and once again retreating into a more private life. When George I died in 1727, the new George II and Queen Caroline were more than happy to continue renovating Hampton Court. The rooms known today as the Cumberland Rooms were built in 1732 for their second son, the Duke of Cumberland, and were designed by William Kent. As it turned out, they were the last rooms to be built at Hampton Court for a member of the royal family.

The full English court visited Hampton Court for the last time in 1737 when Caroline died on 20 November. It was the end of Hampton Court's role as a working royal palace entertaining a full court. After George II died in 1760, his grandson, George III, made it plain that he had no interest in Hampton Court. Apparently this was because George II had once boxed his ears in the state apartments. A resident staff of 40, including the landscape gardener, 'Capability' Brown, looked after the palace, but its furniture and other treasures were gradually transferred to other royal palaces. Many apartments were assigned, rent-free, as grace-and-favour apartments to people who had given great service to king or country. This system operated until the 1970s, although many people who help to run Hampton Court still live there.

Fire and restoration
Hampton Court may have fallen out of royal favour but it was still of great interest to architects and historians. Restoration work was carried out between 1838 and 1851, with several areas of the palace stripped of

their 'improvements' and restored to their original Tudor appearance. Another phase of restoration work took place between 1875 and 1900, again concentrating on the Tudor areas of the palace. The palace was opened to the public in 1838, although not for the first time: in the 16th century Elizabeth I had also allowed paying visitors to view some areas of the palace.

On 31 March 1986, fire broke out in a grace-and-favour apartment on the third floor of the wing containing the King's Apartments. Timber and molten lead fell into the apartments below, causing immense damage to the Cartoon Gallery and King's Privy Chamber. It took six years to repair them, but it was an opportunity to restore them to their original appearance. Whenever possible, this was done using traditional techniques and materials that would have been familiar to Sir Christopher Wren, the chief architect at the time.

Hampton Court today

Hampton Court now resembles a small city with its beautifully arranged courtyards, ancient courts, rooms and staircases. It covers almost 3 hectares (7 acres) of land and 24 hectares (60 acres) of garden. Each section of the palace has its own distinct atmosphere, from the relatively plain rooms of Henry VIII's state apartments to the intimacy of the Queen's private apartments, built for Mary II.

Many ceilings in the palace apartments, whether ribbed Tudor ceilings, baroque plasterwork or adorned with paintings (such as those in the Queen's Apartments), are ornate and very beautiful. When the Duke of Württemberg visited the palace in 1590, he described it as 'the most splendid and most magnificent royal palace of any that may be found in England, or indeed in any other Kingdom.'

ⓘ information

Contact details

Hampton Court Palace
East Molesey
Surrey
KT8 9AU

0844 482 7777 (from the UK)
+44 (0)20 3166 6000 (from outside the UK)

Historic Royal Palaces site
www.hrp.org.uk/hamptoncourtpalace

Transport links

Hampton Court

Routes 111, 216, 411, 451, R68 and 513

Located on the A308, it is well signposted from all major roads

Riverboats run in summer from Westminster, Richmond upon Thames and Kingston upon Thames

HAMPTON COURT PALACE 35

KEW PALACE
Surrey

Located in the magnificent grounds of the Royal Botanical Gardens at Kew near Richmond, Kew Palace began life in the late 17th century as the home of a rich Flemish merchant, Samuel Fortrey. After passing through the hands of several wealthy owners, the handsome four-storey, red-brick villa caught the eye of Queen Caroline, the consort of George II (r. 1727–60), in 1729. The palace was used as a schoolhouse by George III, but became a royal residence again in 1801 and was the final home of Queen Charlotte just 17 years later. Opened to the public by Queen Victoria in 1898, today Kew Palace and its gardens are a popular destination for tourists.

From humble origins

Samuel Fortrey built his country residence in 1631 on the site where one of Elizabeth I's courtiers had lived. An eccentric but engaging building, it was constructed of carved red brick laid in a style known as 'Flemish bond'. Its three-gabled front gave the house a Dutch feel, resulting in it being called the Dutch House. The owners' initials ('S' for Samuel and 'C' for Catherine, his wife) are engraved above the main entrance. The house remained in the Fortrey family for another generation before being sold on. By the end of the 17th century it was owned by Sir Richard Levett, Lord Mayor of London.

Kew had long been a favoured place of the monarchy and it became more so under the reign of George II,

KEY DATES

- 1631 Samuel Fortrey begins building the Dutch House
- 1728 George II leases the house for his three daughters
- 1731 Frederick, Prince of Wales, leases Kew House and uses Kew Palace as the private school and independent household of his sons
- 1781 George III purchases Kew House for his wife, Queen Charlotte
- 1788–9 George III confined to Kew House
- 1800–1810 Used as a summer retreat by the king and his family
- 1818 Queen Charlotte dies there on 17 November and the house is abandoned
- 1898 Opened to the public by Queen Victoria
- 2006 Elizabeth II celebrates her 80th birthday there

▶ *Kew Palace is the most intimate of all the royal residences. It was once known as the Dutch House.*

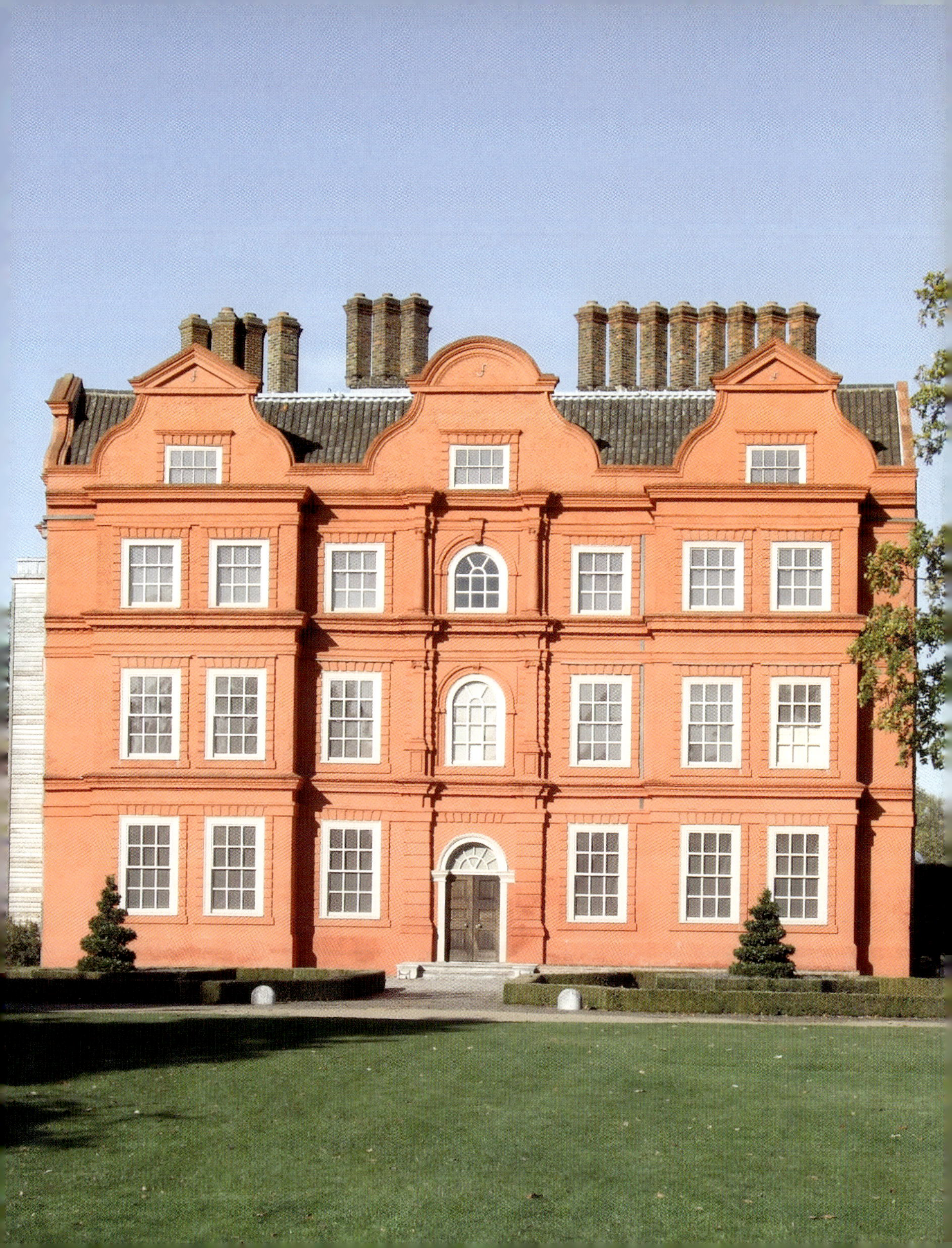

INTERESTING FEATURES

✠ *Carved red brick exterior*

✠ *Garden featuring original plants*

✠ *Jigsaw cabinet featuring the earliest jigsaws*

✠ *Library, where George III kept an impressive collection of books*

✠ *Madame Tussaud bust of George III*

✠ *Queen Charlotte's chair*

✠ *Queen Charlotte's House nearby*

who brought his large family to enjoy the sights there and resided at Richmond Lodge at the southern end of Kew Gardens. Inevitably, the Dutch House caught the couple's attention, and George leased it for their three eldest daughters in 1728. George's son, Frederick, Prince of Wales, lived opposite the Dutch House in the White House (Kew House) and for a time used it as a school room for his sons, the future George III and his brother, Edward.

Frederick commissioned the great architect William Kent and builder William Chambers to remodel the house and lay the foundations of a botanical garden featuring great and exotic plants. When he died rather suddenly of an infection in 1751, his wife Augusta carried on his work with Chambers and William Aiton, her gardener. By 1763, they had established a spectacular garden.

When Augusta's son, George III, came to the throne in 1760, he joined his young wife Charlotte at Richmond Lodge, where they began their family. In 1781, he bought Kew Palace and later gave it to his sons, Prince George and Prince Frederick, when they reached their majority. Queen Charlotte would often walk in the gardens and picnic with her family.

Mad King George

In 1788, George III was declared 'mad', suffering from what modern historians now think is porphyria. During the months of his illness he was incarcerated at the White House, where he was subjected to leeching, emetics and long periods of time in a straitjacket while his family resided at Kew Palace. He suffered two further attacks in 1801 and 1804 and at both times withdrew to Kew to recover. He would visit Queen Charlotte and his unmarried daughters at Kew Palace.

Despite this unhappy association, the house remained a popular residence with the royal family and they often retreated

▶ *The Queen's Garden at the rear of the palace is in the style of a 17th-century garden and contains only those plants known at that time.*

there during the summer between 1800 and 1810, particularly after 1802 when George III demolished the White House to build the (unfinished) Castellated Palace.

In July 1818, the double wedding of the Dukes of Clarence and Kent took place in the Queen's Drawing Room, and later that year, on 17 November, Queen Charlotte died in her bedroom. Visitors can see the chair in which she spent most of her final days. Queen Victoria also requested that her bedroom be kept as it had been during her grandmother's lifetime.

Queen Victoria gave the palace new life by opening it to the public in 1898. It remained open until 1996 when it closed for substantial renovation. When it reopened in 2006, it had been restored to resemble the house as it was when it was most in use by George III and his family.

Visitors can view the dolls' house made by his children, Princess Elizabeth's first-floor bedroom and the bedrooms of Princess Augusta and Princess Amelia.

In 2006, the palace also hosted its first dinner for a monarch in 200 years when Elizabeth II celebrated her 80th birthday there.

ⓘ information

Contact details

Kew Palace
Royal Botanic Gardens Kew
Richmond
Surrey
TW9 3AB

☎ 0844 482 7777 (from UK); +44 (0)20 3166 6000 (from outside the UK)

Historic Royal Palaces site
www.hrp.org.uk/kewpalace

Transport links

Kew Bridge or Kew Gardens

Kew Gardens

65, 237, 267 (summer Sundays only) and 391

In summer from Westminster, Richmond upon Thames and Kingston upon Thames

HEVER CASTLE
Kent

During its 800-year history, Hever Castle has belonged to two of the most powerful families in Britain. During the 16th century, Hever was home to the Bullen family, most of whose members were climbing the social ladder at Henry VIII's court. In the early 20th century, Hever became the domain of William Waldorf Astor, the American multi-millionaire, who transformed it from a near ruin to the picturesque castle surrounded by gardens, a lake and a Tudor village that we know today.

A rise to power

The oldest parts of Hever are the gatehouse, outer walls and moat; the De Hever family, who also gave their name to their new home, built these in 1270. When Sir Geoffrey Bullen, Lord Mayor of London, acquired the castle around 1460, he built a house within the outer walls. The Bullens prospered; Sir Geoffrey's grandson, Sir Thomas, was an ambitious courtier who had the ear of Henry VIII. This was partly due to Thomas's marriage to Elizabeth Howard, the daughter of the 2nd Duke of Norfolk. Having achieved a powerful position within court, Thomas was anxious to consolidate it; he pushed forward his three surviving children, Mary, George and Anne, to ensure that they were always at the centre of royal attention. In 1522, Anne, having changed her surname from Bullen to Boleyn, was appointed lady-

KEY DATES

- 1270 Gatehouse, outer walls and moat built by the De Hever family
- c.1460 Castle acquired by Sir Geoffrey Bullen
- 1491 Prince Henry (later Henry VIII) born on 28 June
- 1522 Anne Boleyn appointed lady-in-waiting to Catherine of Aragon
- 1533 Secret marriage of Henry VIII and Anne Boleyn on 25 January
- 1533 Anne Boleyn crowned Queen Consort on 1 June
- 1536 Execution of Anne Boleyn on 19 May
- 1903 Hever Castle bought by William Waldorf Astor
- 1963 The castle and gardens opened to the public for the first time
- 1983 Hever Castle and its estate sold to Broadland Properties Ltd

▶ *The gardens are one of the delights at Hever Castle. In addition to the many examples of topiary, there is a maze, an Italian garden, a rhododendron walk and a water maze.*

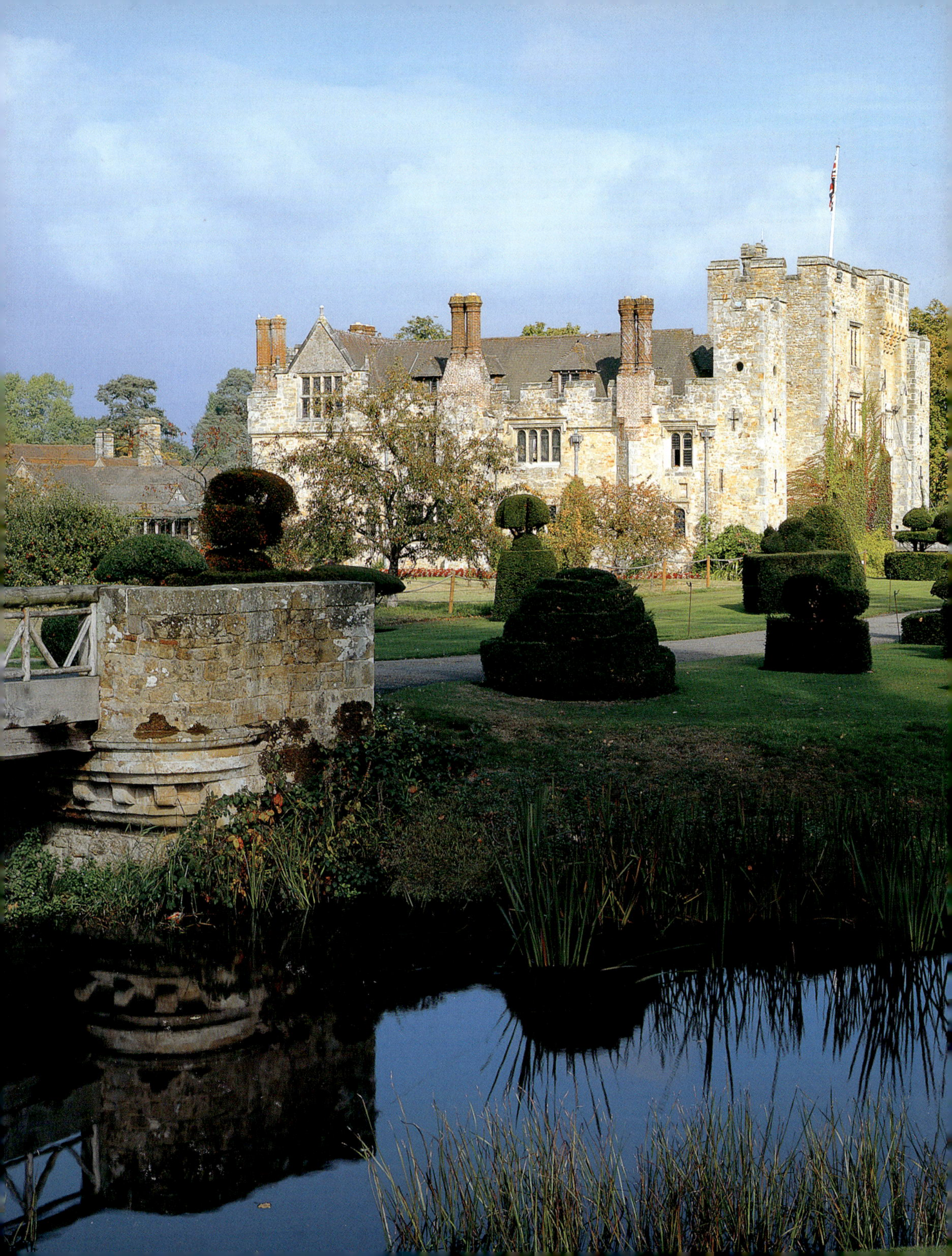

INTERESTING FEATURES

- The Inner Courtyard
- The Inner Hall
- The Drawing Room
- The Entrance Hall
- The door locks in the Dining Room
- The Library
- The Morning Room
- The Maze

in-waiting to Henry VIII's wife, Catherine of Aragon, thereby triggering the start of one of English history's most famous and

▼ *The Dining Hall is one of the rooms that was expertly restored between 1903 and 1906 while under William Astor's ownership.*

momentous phases. Not only was it a powerful love story, it also heralded the end of the Pope's influence over England and the beginning of the Church of England, presided over by the reigning monarch. Anne, like Catherine, was unable to produce a surviving male heir; the only living child was a girl, Princess Elizabeth.

Henry had removed Anne from the throne with a manufactured charge of high treason for adultery with four men and incest with her brother, George, who was executed two days before Anne in May 1536. The Bullen family's star had now crashed. Two years later, both Anne's parents were dead and Hever Castle was taken over by Henry, who gave it to his fourth wife, Anne of Cleves, as part of her divorce settlement.

William Waldorf Astor

Hever Castle's second incursion into the history books occurred at the turn of the 20th century, when William Waldorf Astor bought it. His family had made a fortune in America and he was now happily spending it in Britain, having declared that his native country was 'no longer a fit place for a gentleman to live'. One of his most ambitious projects was to rescue Hever from its wretched and ruinous condition. He completely restored the building in the most painstaking fashion, landscaped the gardens, excavated the lake and provided guest accommodation by building a Tudor village. Although this appears to be a collection of individual Tudor cottages built at different times by different people, they were, in fact, all constructed at the same time and many of the buildings are linked internally. The village contains over 100 rooms, many of which are now available for corporate events.

William Waldorf Astor restored Hever so beautifully that it is difficult to detect any signs of modern conveniences, such as electric light switches. The rooms have been furnished to reflect their surroundings using furniture from a variety of different periods – rather than exclusively Tudor – to give the castle an eclectic, interesting atmosphere. Some of the rooms, such as the library, even have the feel of a comfortable family home rather than something more suited to a museum.

information

Contact details

Estate Office
Hever Castle
Hever
Near Edenbridge
Kent TN8 7NG

+44 (0)1732 865224

Hever Castle official site
www.hevercastle.co.uk

Transport links

Edenbridge Town station (then taxi)

30 minutes from Gatwick; 1 hour from Heathrow, then car or train

5 km (3 miles) south-east of Edenbridge off the B2026 between Sevenoaks and East Grinstead

LEEDS CASTLE
Kent

KEY DATES

✠ **857** Ledian builds Esledes Manor

✠ **c.1119** Robert de Crevecoeur builds a stone motte and bailey fortification

✠ **1278** Edward I makes Leeds a royal residence

✠ **1328** Edward II besieges the castle

✠ **1520** Henry VIII stops at Leeds Castle on his way to the Field of the Cloth of Gold tournament

✠ **1552** The castle passes into private hands

✠ **1926** Lady Baillie buys Leeds Castle

✠ **1974** The Leeds Castle Foundation comes into existence

Set in 500 acres, Leeds Castle is a magnificent building with a long history spanning more than 900 years. The castle is located near Maidstone, in the heartland of Kent, in southern England, and was named after Ledian, chief minister of Ethelbert IV (r. 856–860). Originally a Saxon fortress built on two small islands, it is listed in the Domesday Book and has undergone great change over the centuries. It was an essential part of Norman fortifications during Norman times, a royal residence under Edward I, the home of six queens and a royal palace of Henry VIII.

Once called the 'loveliest castle in the world' by Lord Conway, Leeds became the royal residence of Edward I and Eleanor of Castile in 1278. The king built a royal chapel to conduct daily mass and undertook major renovations, including adding the Barbican (made up of three parts, each with its own separate entrance, drawbridge, gateway and portcullis). In honour of Queen Eleanor, the medieval keep of the castle, which incorporates the Great Hall, was called 'Gloriette'. Henry VIII later added to this structure.

Anne of Bohemia, Joan of Navarre and Catherine de Valois all lived at the castle, and Henry VIII brought Catherine of Aragon there on his way to meet Francis I at the Field of the Cloth of Gold tournament in France in 1520. This is depicted in a painting in the Banqueting Hall. Henry also added many Tudor windows as part of his conversion of the fortified castle into a royal palace.

From royal to private hands

The castle remained in royal hands until 1552, when Edward VI granted it to a courtier for services rendered. It then remained in private hands. The St Legers, the Culpepers, and later the Fairfaxes and the Wykeham-Martins, resided there, and in 1926 the latter sold it to Anglo–American heiress Lady Baillie. She restored it to its former glory and built up a fine collection of ceramics, paintings, tapestries and furniture.

▲ *Originally a Saxon fortress built on two small islands, Leeds Castle has undergone great renovation over the centuries.*

INTERESTING FEATURES

- *The medieval Gatehouse*
- *The Gloriette built by Edward I*
- *The gardens*

information

Contact details

Leeds Castle
Maidstone, Kent
ME17 1PL

+44 (0)1622 765 400

Leeds Castle
www.leeds-castle.com

Transport links

Bearsted. A coach shuttle service run by Spot Hire is available from the station

11 km (7 miles) east of Maidstone, junction 8 of the M20 motorway

LEEDS CASTLE

THE ROYAL PAVILION
Brighton, Sussex

KEY DATES

✠ 1784 The Prince of Wales rents Grove House for the summer

✠ 1785 The Prince and Mrs Maria Fitzherbert are secretly married on 19 September

✠ 1795 The Prince's official marriage to Princess Caroline of Brunswick on 8 April

✠ 1787–1822 Marine Pavilion is gradually transformed into the Royal Pavilion

✠ 1817–20 The music and banqueting rooms are built by John Nash

✠ 1818 The great dome over the Saloon is constructed by John Nash

✠ 1821 The Prince Regent is crowned George IV on 19 July

✠ 1821 Gasolier in the Banqueting Room is first lit by gas in December

✠ 1830 Death of George IV on 26 June

✠ 1849 Royal Pavilion bought by the town of Brighton

Of all the people that have made up the British royal family in the past thousand years, few have provoked more criticism and dislike than the Prince Regent, who became George IV in 1820. He was notorious in his day for his extravagance, licentiousness, self-indulgence and wild flights of fancy. Contemporary cartoonists, such as James Gilray and George Cruikshank, delighted in producing scabrous and vicious comments on his musicianship, love life, portly figure, clothes, spending habits and anything else they felt was fair game. William Thackeray, writing about him in *The Four Georges*, said: 'I try to take him to pieces, and find silk stockings, padding, stays, a coat with frogs and a fur collar, and star and blue ribbon, a pocket-handkerchief prodigiously scented, one of Truefitt's best nutty-brown wigs reeking with oil, a set of teeth and a huge black stock, underwaistcoats, more underwaistcoats, and then nothing.'

What Thackeray failed to mention is the magnificent cultural legacy that George IV left behind. His Regency period saw a host of artistic achievements, one of the greatest of which was undoubtedly his own Royal Pavilion in Brighton. This astonishing phantasmagoria of domes, minarets and tented roofs was the pet project of the Prince of Wales for almost 20 years, and a showcase for the talents of the architects Henry Holland and John Nash. The interior of the Pavilion was

▶ *The Royal Pavilion is a stone's throw from the sea – the real reason why the Prince Regent wanted to pursue his experiment of living like a private gentleman in Brighton.*

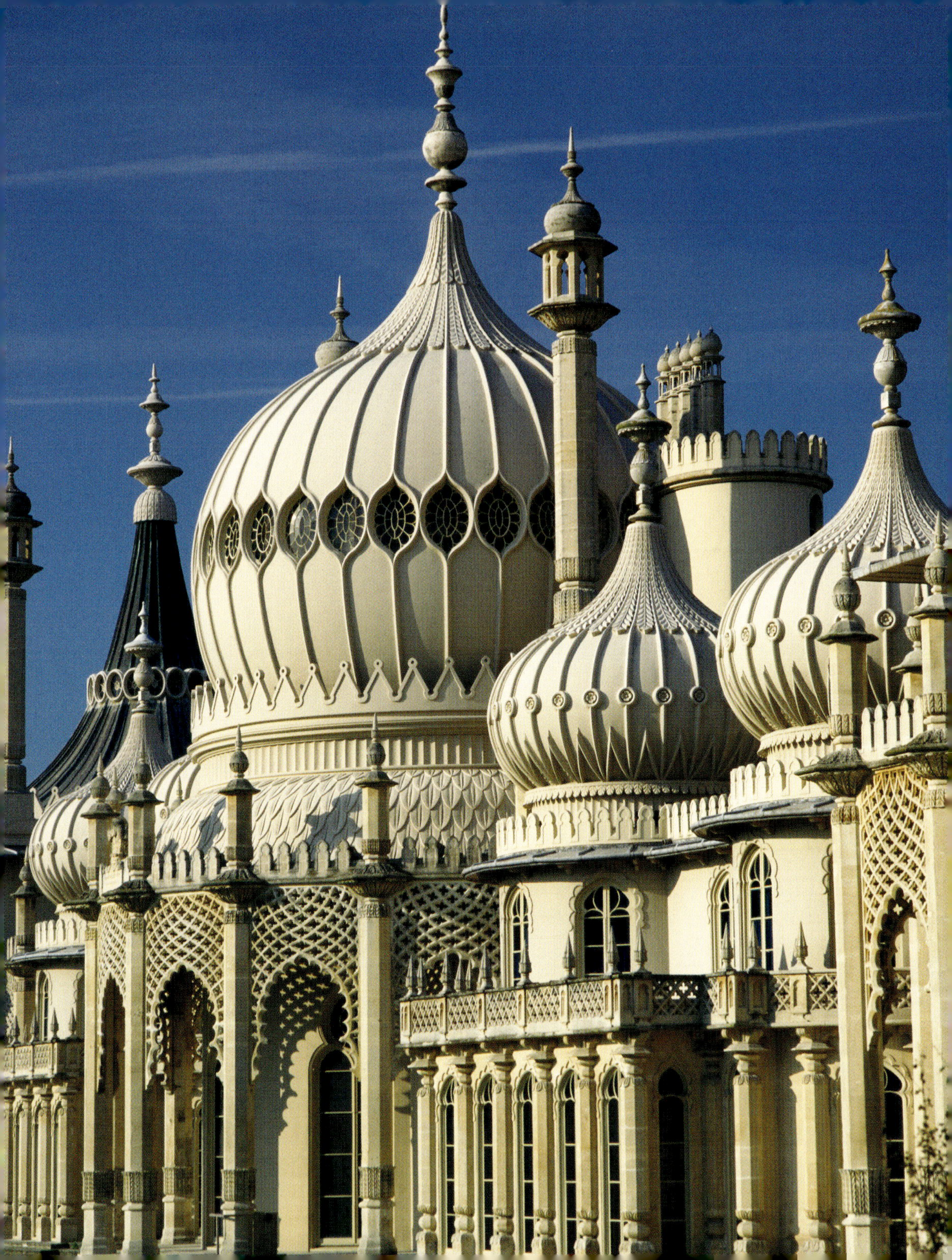

breathtaking in its extravagance and decoration, even in a lavish era.

Extravagance and debt

In the 1780s, Brighthelmstone, as Brighton was then known, was highly fashionable and said by the *Morning Herald* to be 'the Paris of its day'. Sea bathing was the rage. The town also enjoyed royal patronage from the Duke of Cumberland, brother of George III. When the Prince of Wales visited his uncle there in 1783, he was captivated and took Grove House, where the Music Room of the Pavilion now stands, for the season the following year. Already, at the age of 22, he was £250,000 in debt, having spent a fortune on renovating Carlton House in London. He was unable to budget or control his spending and didn't see why he should. His father, George III, refused to help unless the Prince of Wales gave a full account of all his debts, but this was not an acceptable proposal for the prince. Work stopped on Carlton House and he announced that he had decided to live like a private gentleman in Brighton. He leased a farmhouse, Brighton House, between the Castle Inn and Grove House.

Marine Pavilion

The prince loved renovating houses and it was not long before Henry Holland, the architect who had worked on Carlton House, was summoned to Brighton. By 1788, Brighton House was known as the Marine Pavilion and had undergone the first

> ### INTERESTING FEATURES
> - *The faux bamboo in the corridor*
> - *The intricately decorated domed ceiling and gasolier in the Banqueting Room*
> - *The rows of copper pans in the Great Kitchen*
> - *The Mughal style of the mirrors in the Saloon*
> - *The Chinese dragon motifs in the Music Room*

of many transformations: a rotunda, bow windows and an oriental dome were added, although most of the exterior was still quite plain. The prince's private life had also been transformed, as he had secretly married Maria Fitzherbert, a young Catholic widow, in 1785. This was in direct contravention of the Royal Marriages Act of 1772 designed to prevent members of the royal family making unsuitable or scandalous marriages; the marriage of a Protestant heir to the British throne to a Catholic widow came under both categories, and was therefore invalid. However, Mrs Fitzherbert was a good influence on the prince, curbing many of his excesses while making him happy. The couple were generous and popular patrons of Brighton, but by the early 1790s the marriage was foundering. The prince had been enticed away by the wily Lady Jersey, a member of the court, and was once again heavily in debt. With little option, he made a deal with Parliament and agreed to an arranged marriage in 1795 with his first cousin, Caroline of Brunswick, in return for Parliament paying off his debts.

A failed marriage

Almost as soon as it began, this proved to be an unhappy marriage, with each party profoundly disappointed by the unprepossessing appearance of the other – although not before Princess Caroline had conceived a child on their wedding night.

The estranged couple continued to keep up appearances in public, as the prospect of a royal divorce was unthinkable. Their private life, however, was a state of war, a situation not helped by Lady Jersey, who was still the prince's mistress as well as Caroline's lady-in-waiting. Further disappointment arrived when Caroline's baby was born a girl. By 1800, with his relationship with Lady Jersey over and his marriage in shreds, the prince successfully persuaded Mrs Fitzherbert to return to him. She only conceded after securing a papal confirmation of the canonical validity of her marriage to him. Once again, she became a good and restraining influence on the Prince. They lived together very happily for eight years.

▶ *The Prince Regent entertained on a lavish scale. The Banqueting Hall was the first room to be illuminated and heated by gas.*

Enlargements and extensions

Brighton, in the meantime, had become a mini-court and Henry Holland was asked to extend and alter the Pavilion. It was at this point that the Chinese style, so pronounced at the Pavilion, appeared. Chinoiserie, a European decorative art form influenced by China, had been all the rage in the second half of the 18th century but was no longer de rigueur in fashionable domestic houses. However, the prince sparked a revival.

In 1812, James Wyatt, the Crown's surveyor-general, was commissioned to enlarge the Pavilion at an estimated cost of £100,000. However, he died in 1813 and John Nash was asked to take over. Nash, already an accomplished architect, was used to working for royalty and the aristocracy. He had rebuilt Royal Lodge in Windsor Park in 1813 as a cottage orné, and was working on rooms at Carlton House at the time of the commission. Some of Nash's work on the Pavilion was revolutionary. The Great Dome over the Saloon, for example, built in 1818, was a feat of engineering; the prince even made a special journey from London to see it erected. The original structure was not strong enough to support the weight of the dome, so Nash built a huge iron cage, on which the dome could rest, around the exterior walls. In 1819 further exterior adornments – minarets, small domes and columns made of Bath stone – were added. Unfortunately, the ironwork for the cages and the cores in the small minarets eventually started to rust and expand, causing many problems.

Although there were plans to build to the southwest of the pavilion, Nash's work was almost over by the end of 1820. There was a brief rift between Nash and the prince, by now King George IV, when the mastic stucco on the roofs began to let in water, which caused much damage over the years. The tent roofs above the Music and Banqueting Rooms were eventually recovered in copper in 1827.

William IV

As he grew older, George IV's health declined. He was plagued by dropsy and gout, and neither condition was helped by his considerable size and enthusiasm for wine. He was also a victim of the success he had made of Brighton. He became unnerved by the inquisitive crowds that plagued him there

◀ *The Great Kitchen was a marvel: a highly efficient kitchen decorated in the style of the Pavilion, with copper palm trees topping the cast-iron columns.*

and his last visit was in 1827. Ever the enthusiastic renovator, however, he was not idle in London and kept busy refurbishing Windsor Castle and Buckingham Palace. When George IV died in 1830, Brighton collectively held its breath. Although his brother had had his own apartment within the Pavilion when he was Duke of Clarence, would he still patronize it now that he was king? Thankfully, yes.

Brighton gave a triumphal welcome to William IV and Queen Adelaide. More building work ensued, creating rooms for visitors and servants, with John Nash now acting as advisor and the work carried out by the architect Joseph Good. William IV had neither the taste nor the imagination of George IV, believing that houses should be as plain as possible, but he enjoyed his visits to the Pavilion and left the decorations intact.

William's successor, Queen Victoria, did not spend much time at the Pavilion, preferring to remove much of its contents to Buckingham Palace. Besides, it was too vivid a reminder of her 'wicked uncles'. In 1846 it was announced that the Pavilion was to be sold in order to pay for the extensions to Buckingham Palace. The contents were systematically removed to other royal palaces, but despite a parliamentary proposal that the Pavilion be demolished and the land used without restriction the town of Brighton decided to buy it in 1849.

The Pavilion was gradually restored to its former splendour, with Queen Victoria returning most of the decorations in 1863. It went through a curious period in the First World War when it was used as a military hospital, but Queen Mary, the grand-niece of George IV, took an active interest in its welfare from 1912 onwards. The Pavilion again went into decline during the Second World War, after which there was more talk of demolition. Since then, there has been increasing interest in the splendours of the Pavilion, and painstaking restoration work has continued on this rich architectural fantasia, a fitting memorial to George IV.

information

Contact details

The Royal Pavilion
4/5 Pavilion Buildings
Brighton BN1 1EE

+44 (0)3000 290900

Royal Pavilion, Museum and Libraries
www.brighton-hove-rpml.org.uk/RoyalPavilion/Pages/home.aspx

Transport links

Brighton (then a 15-minute walk)

30 minutes by road or rail from Gatwick Airport

96 km (60 miles) from London; take the M25 then south along the M23 and A23

THE ROYAL PAVILION

ROYAL OSBORNE
Isle of Wight

KEY DATES

✠ 1845 Queen Victoria and Prince Albert buy Osborne House

✠ 1845–51 The new Osborne House is built by architect Thomas Cubitt

✠ 1854 The Swiss cottage is given by Victoria to her children on 24 May

✠ 1861 Death of Prince Albert on 14 December

✠ 1876 Queen Victoria declared Empress of India on 1 May

✠ 1890–1 The Durbar wing is added to Osborne House

✠ 1901 Death of Queen Victoria at Osborne House on 22 January

✠ 1902 Osborne House given to the nation by Edward VII

Queen Victoria and her husband, Prince Albert, bought Osborne House on the Isle of Wight in October 1845. It seemed the perfect choice for the private home they were searching for, away from the rigours of court life.

The Royal Pavilion at Brighton had been mooted as a prospective home at one stage, but Queen Victoria dismissed it because she did not like the building, and also because Brighton had become such a busy tourist destination that it offered little chance of the seclusion Victoria and Albert desired. Victoria, always prone to impulses prompted by nostalgia, was interested in buying a house on the Isle of Wight because she had enjoyed two summer holidays there as a young girl.

Osborne House and its setting immediately entranced Victoria and Albert. 'It is impossible to imagine a prettier spot', Queen Victoria wrote after visiting Osborne House. It was obvious when they viewed it that the three-storey Georgian house was far too small for the couple's needs, but pulling it down and building something larger would easily remedy that. What really captivated them were the views of the Solent, which reminded Albert of the Bay of Naples in Italy. This was his inspiration for the Italian Renaissance style of the new house and gardens, and work began almost at once.

▶ *The architect Thomas Cubitt was commissioned to demolish the old house, build a pavilion to accommodate the private royal apartments and add on further wings for the royal household.*

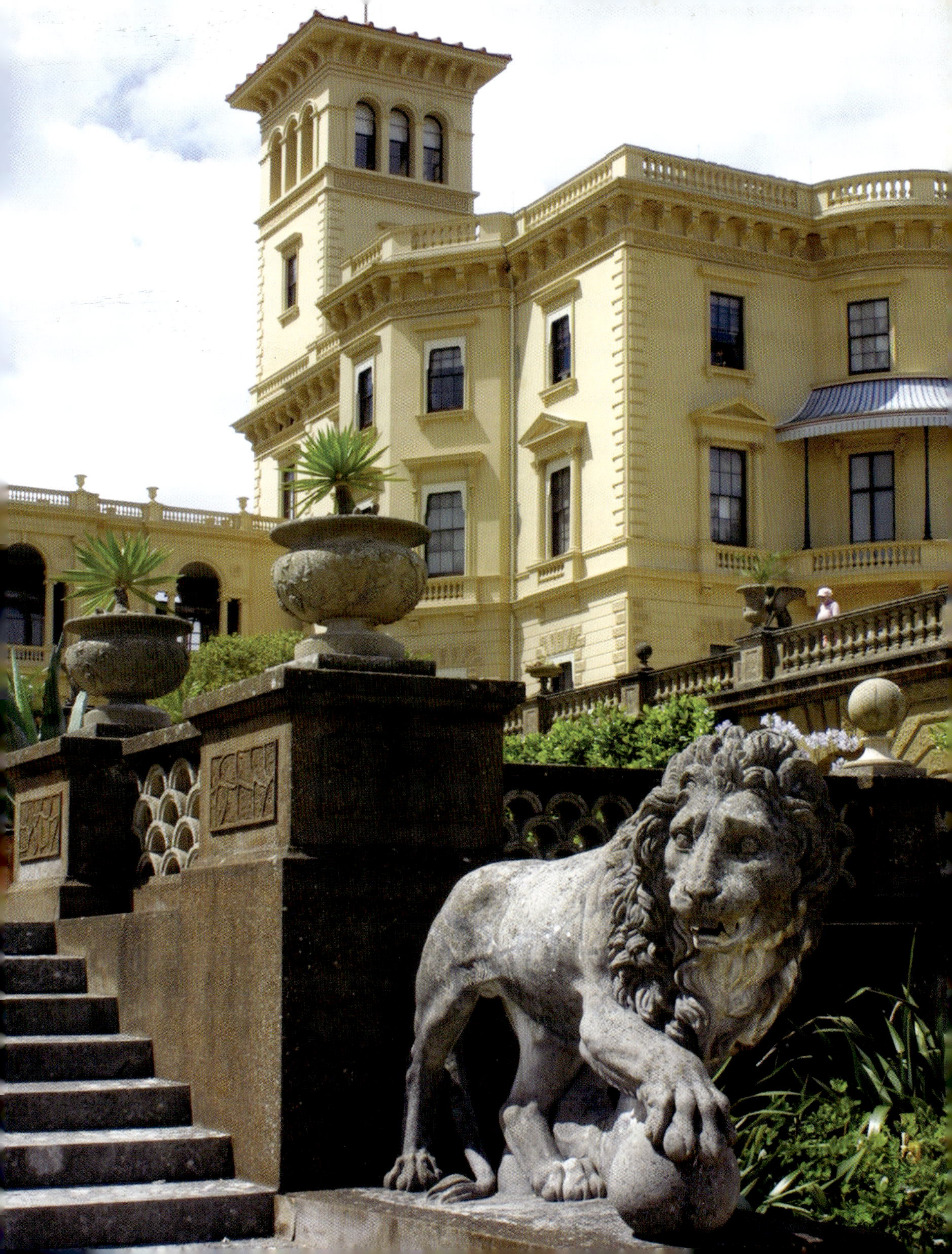

The gardens

The architect for the new house was Thomas Cubitt, who was at the height of his success. His huge team of workmen ensured that the original building was demolished and replaced in as short a time as possible. The gardens were landscaped in suitably Italianate style by Prince Albert in collaboration with Ludwig Grüner, with Albert directing the planting of large specimen trees from his vantage point in one of Osborne's towers. Albert was so caught up in the excitement of creating a private home that he happily planted many of the smaller trees and shrubs himself.

The Swiss cottage

Victoria's gift to her children on her birthday in 1854 was a Swiss cottage, which, as its name implies, was dismantled and brought piece by piece from Switzerland to Osborne House where it was reassembled in the grounds. This was where the children were encouraged to learn to garden. Each child was given a rectangular plot in which to grow fruit, vegetables and flowers. They would then sell their crops to their father to give them a secure grounding in simple economics. They also learned to cook in the Swiss cottage, as it had a fully equipped kitchen. There is something very charming about this desire to keep the children's feet on the ground as, even then, it must have been self-evident that they would all marry into the great European families.

> ### INTERESTING FEATURES
> ✠ *The Durbar Room*
> ✠ *The Billiard Room*
> ✠ *The Dining Room*
> ✠ *The Queen's Sitting Room*
> ✠ *The Queen's Bedroom*
> ✠ *The gardens*
> ✠ *The Swiss cottage*

Domestic idyll

Osborne House became a real home to the royal family. It meant so much to them that even the royal yacht was called *Osborne*. They stayed there each year for four lengthy periods: in spring; for Victoria's birthday in May; in July and August, when they celebrated Albert's birthday; and just before Christmas. They allowed photographers and painters to capture incidents from their family life in the grounds and in the house, partly for their own enjoyment and partly as a form of propaganda to the nation to show what a happy, devoted family they were. Many thousands of prints of the royal family were sold to the public, and Victoria truly believed that 'no Sovereign was ever more loved than I am (I am bold enough to say)'.

Although Osborne was a beloved family home, it was also the home of a queen and her consort, as the lavish interior decorations show. There are also many reminders of Victoria's dynastic links with the other European royal families: the Billiard Room houses a massive porcelain vase, which was a gift from a Russian tsar. The grandeur of the Billiard Room, the Queen's Dining Room and the Drawing

▲ *The fresco on the upper landing was painted by William Dyce in 1847 and is entitled 'Neptune resigning the empire of the seas to Britannia'.*

Room on the ground floor forms a marked contrast with the much more homely and unassuming décor of the royal apartments on the first floor, however. These private

ROYAL OSBORNE 55

Prince Albert played a central role in the landscaping of the Italianate gardens that complement Osborne House.

upper-class family in which parents and children only met once a day for a short period of stilted conversation. Today, there are photographs of the family on Victoria and Albert's desks that reveal more evidence of how they lived as a family.

Osborne in mourning

Sadly, this domestic idyll ended at Windsor Castle on 14 December 1861, when Albert died at the age of 42 from typhoid. Victoria famously went into impenetrable mourning and retreated to Windsor and Osborne with her memories. The private royal apartments were effectively sealed in a time capsule, with everything preserved as it had been when Albert was alive. The couple's domestic routine also continued as though Albert were still there, even to the extent of his shaving things and clothes being laid out for him each day. When she took decisions, Victoria tried to do whatever she believed her sainted Albert would have done in the same circumstances. She revered him to such an extent that the poor man was unfairly considered to be even more of a bore in death than he had been in life.

Such deep, intractable mourning, with its inevitable retreat from her people, almost caused Victoria to lose the throne as it sparked off profound republican sentiments in many corners of her realm. Victoria dedicated

rooms, which include the Prince's Dressing Room, the Queen's Sitting Room, the Queen's Bedroom and the children's nurseries, were intended for private, domestic use, and were therefore as comfortable as possible. Victoria and Albert wanted to bring up their children in as natural and loving an environment as their situation allowed so the young princes and princesses often visited their parents' bedrooms; this was not the sort of Victorian

herself to erecting monuments to Albert's memory at every opportunity but, apart from that, she chose to stay out of the public gaze for ten years. She described herself as 'a poor weak woman shattered by grief and anxiety'.

Empress of India

It took years for Victoria to return fully to public life, a process she carried out by degrees. One of the greatest incentives was celebrated at Osborne in the opulent Durbar Room. In 1876, Victoria was declared Empress of India, which at the time was one of Britain's most glittering colonial possessions. The Durbar Room was built for state functions, and the wing that contains it was added to Osborne House between 1890 and 1891. The room's name is an anglicized version of the Hindi word *darbar,* which means 'court'. Bhai Ram Singh decorated the Durbar Room in an elaborate, intricate style, with a carpet from Agra. It now contains the gifts Queen Victoria received on her Golden and Diamond Jubilees in 1887 and 1897 respectively. These include engraved silver and copper vases, Indian armour and a model of an Indian palace.

Victoria's death

Queen Victoria died at Osborne House on 22 January 1901 with two generations of her family gathered around her. Although Victoria had adored it, Osborne held few charms for her children. Victoria's will left strict instructions that the house should stay in the family, but no one wanted it, so Edward VII presented it to the nation. The public was allowed to visit the state apartments, but the private apartments were closed and the rest of the house was used as a Royal Naval college and also as a convalescent home for officers from the army and navy.

Today, Osborne House has been renamed Royal Osborne and extensively refurbished to look as it did in Queen Victoria's time to recapture the feel of the home that she loved so dearly.

ⓘ information

Contact details

Royal Osborne
The Avenue, East Cowes
Isle of Wight, PO32 6JX

+44 (0)1983 200022

English Heritage
www.english-heritage.org.uk/daysout/properties/osborne-house

Transport links

Ryde Espalande, 11 km (7 miles); Wootton, 5 km (3 miles)

East Cowes, 2.5 km (1½ miles); Fishbourne, 6.5 km (4 miles); Ryde, 11 km (7 miles)

1.6 km (1 mile) from East Cowes

CARISBROOKE CASTLE
Isle of Wight

KEY DATES

✠ **1060s** First Norman castle built at Carisbrooke

✠ **1078** The castle forfeited by Roger FitzOsbern to William the Conqueror

✠ **1100** Henry I gives Carisbrooke to the de Redvers family

✠ **1100** Construction of the present castle begins

✠ **1293** Isabella de Redvers sells the castle before her death

✠ **1597–1602** Carisbrooke is given additional fortifications

✠ **1647–8** Charles I is imprisoned at Carisbrooke Castle

✠ **1896** Princess Beatrice becomes governor of the castle

Several royal palaces in Britain began life in private ownership but were later acquired by the reigning sovereign as punishment for a transgression by the owner. Carisbrooke Castle on the Isle of Wight is a classic example of this.

Passing into royal hands

The position of Carisbrooke Castle, just off the south coast of England in the English Channel, has for centuries made the Isle of Wight a prime strategic point for foreign invaders. If they could land here and secure the island, they had the perfect launch for their final bid to invade England. This point was not lost on the Normans, who invaded England in 1066: they knew that if they could do this, so could other invading armies, and they therefore needed to defend their newly won land with a string of fortresses. There was already a Saxon fort at Carisbrooke, occupying a perfect position on high ground and close to the River Medina, so the Norman lord, William FitzOsbern, built a wooden fort on top of the old Saxon defences.

It was FitzOsbern's son, Roger, who took part in a rebellion against William the Conqueror in 1078 and had to forfeit all his lands as punishment. Although the castle was now in royal hands, it was once again used as a base for insurrection when, in 1082, William's half-brother, Odo, staged another rebellion against him. In 1100, Henry I gave the castle to the de Redvers family

▶ *The Norman Gateway, which was heavily defended to repel possible invaders, leads into the courtyard of the castle.*

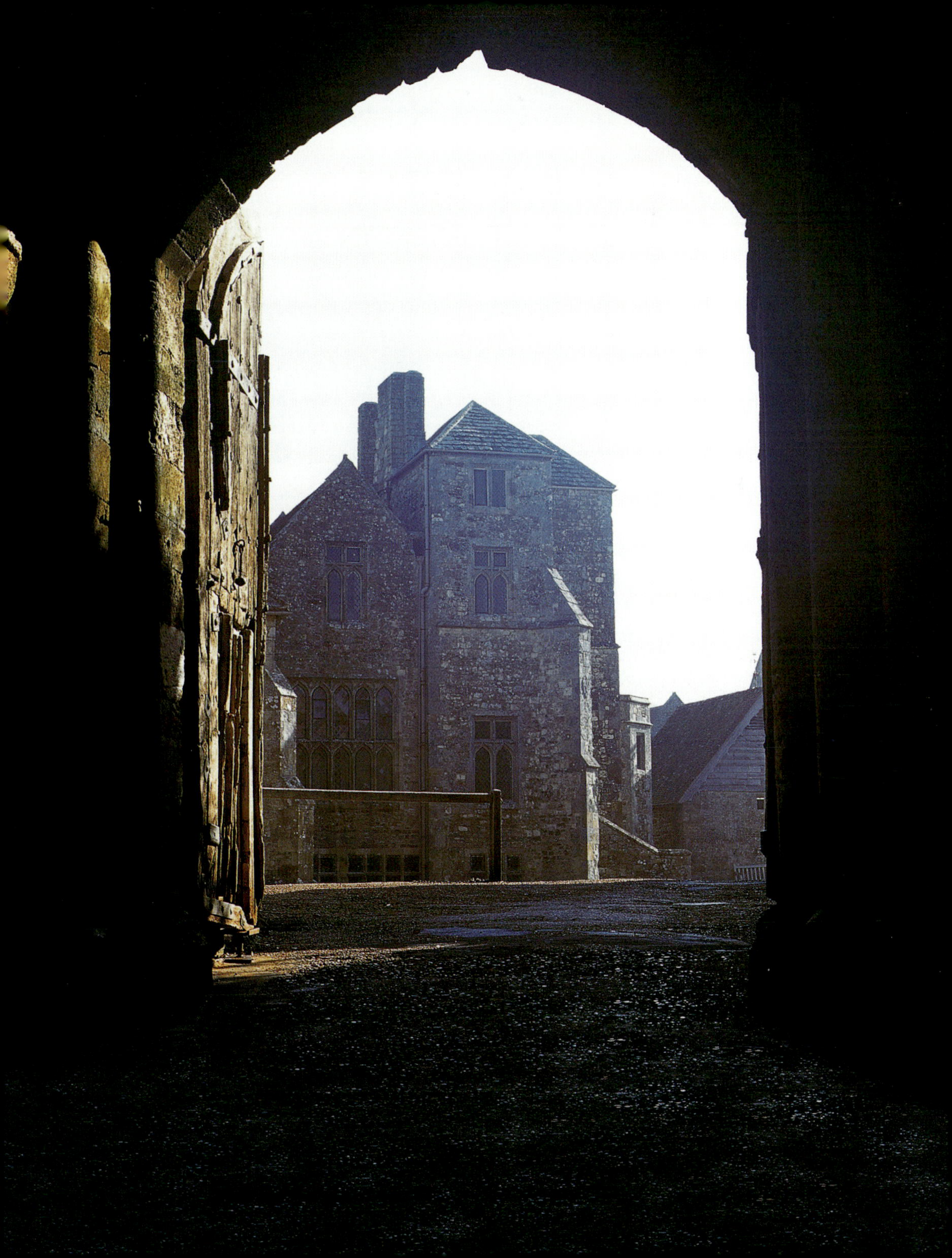

and also made them lords of the Isle of Wight. They began to build the stone castle that stands here today, and Carisbrooke stayed in their family until 1293 when the last owner and lord, Isabella, sold it to the Bishop of Durham, who bought it on behalf of Edward I. Isabella enjoyed a high level of comfort at Carisbrooke, even to the extent of having glass in the windows, which was an almost unheard of luxury at the time because of the excessive cost involved. The castle was besieged in 1377 by an invading French army, which was eventually beaten back after its commander was killed by a single arrow fired from one of the arrow slits in the castle walls.

Increasing the fortifications

Medieval Britain was a turbulent country, so it was important to keep defensive castles such as Carisbrooke in good condition in case they were needed in a hurry. After the national emergency triggered by the threat of the Spanish Armada in 1588, Elizabeth I carried out works between 1597 and 1602 to make sure that Carisbrooke was adequately fortified.

▼ *The courtyard inside the castle contains many buildings, including the governor's quarters (left) and the Well House (right).*

In an ironic twist of fate, the fortifications paid for by Elizabeth I were eventually used against her cousin, Charles I. In November 1647, during the English Civil War, Charles I decided to escape the dangerous atmosphere of London for what he thought was the safety of the Isle of Wight. Much to his astonishment, and what must have been considerable displeasure for a king who truly believed that he was a god in human form, the governor of Carisbrooke Castle took Charles into custody and held him prisoner there until September 1648. Legend has it that Charles tried to escape by crawling through a window, but the spacing between the mullions was too small and he became stuck. His daughter, Elizabeth, was also held prisoner at the castle and died there on 8 September 1650.

As the centuries progressed, Carisbrooke was allowed to decline into a ruin. Nevertheless, the castle gained another royal patron in 1896 when Princess Beatrice, the youngest daughter of Queen Victoria (and who went through her very long life with the nickname 'Baby'), became governor of Carisbrooke and restored it as best she could. She introduced the first museum at the castle, proving that she had inherited her mother's love for the past and her determination to preserve Britain's royal palaces. In recognition of her work, a new Princess Beatrice Garden has recently been planted in the grounds of the castle.

INTERESTING FEATURES

- *The window through which Charles I tried to escape*
- *The defensive earthworks created in the 16th century*
- *The museum*
- *The Norman stone keep on top of the motte*

information

Contact details

Carisbrooke Castle
Castle Hill, Newport
Isle of Wight, PO30 1XY

+44 (0)1983 522107

English Heritage site
www.english-heritage.org.uk/daysout/properties/carisbrooke-castle

Transport links

West Cowes, 8 km (5 miles), East Cowes, 9.5 km (6 miles); Fishbourne, 9.5 km (6 miles), Ryde, 13 km (8 miles)

2 km (1¼ miles) south-west of Newport. Follow signs for Carisbrooke village and castle

London

From the delights of the Queen's House in Greenwich to the grandeur of Buckingham Palace, London is rich in royal residences. There is something to suit every aesthetic taste, whether it is for the purity of Romanesque architecture or the complexities of Victorian Gothic. Some of the buildings, including St James's Palace, continue to be working palaces in which the business of state is conducted daily, while others, such as Eltham Palace, are now tourist destinations. London's oldest palace, which was originally built as a fortress, is the Tower of London – one of the most famous buildings in the world.

▶ *One of the best views of the Tower of London is from the River Thames. The Tower has grown over the centuries according to the whims and needs of successive monarchs.*

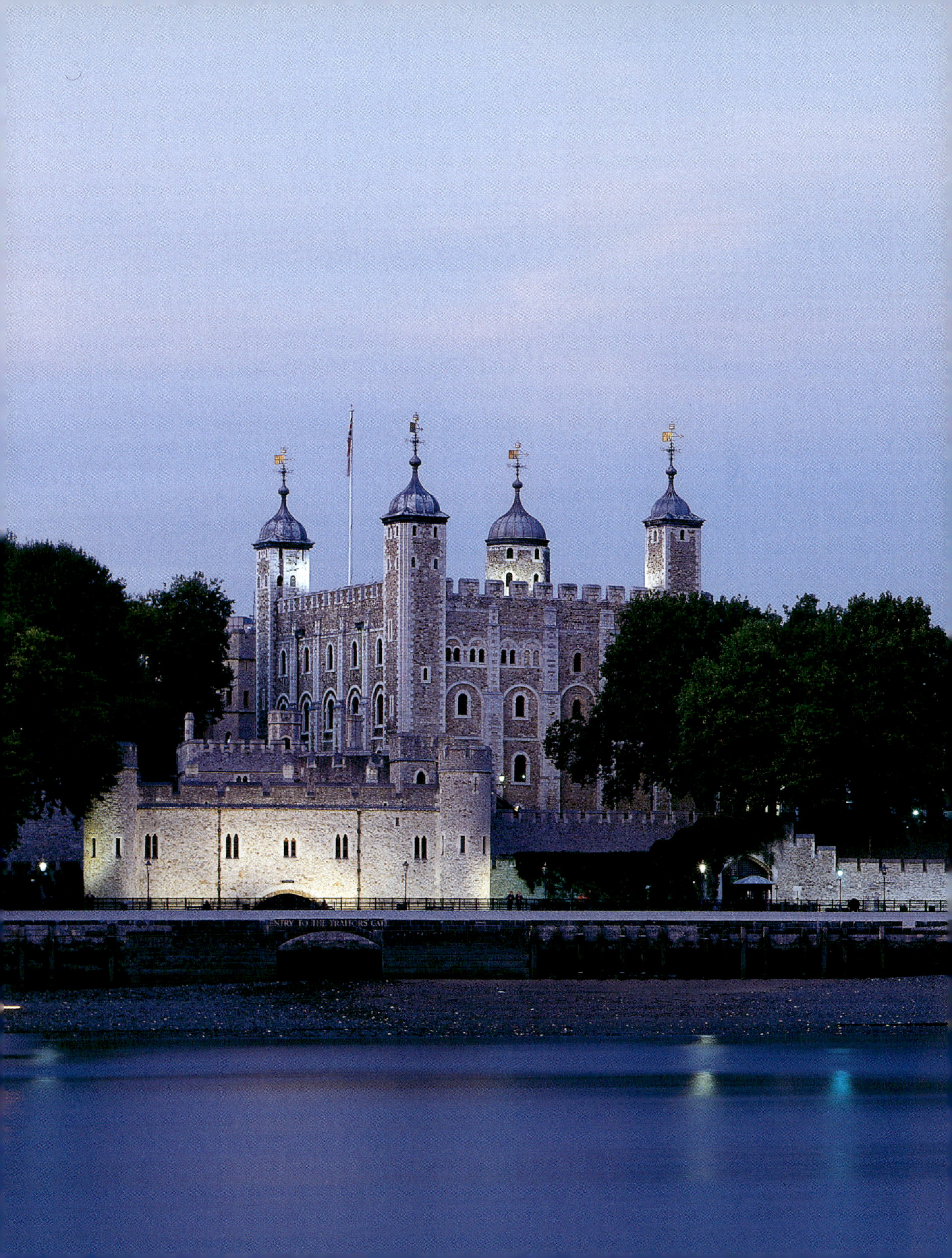

BUCKINGHAM PALACE
London

KEY DATES

- 1633 Goring House built
- 1761 Buckingham House bought as the London home of George III
- 1762–74 Remodelling of Buckingham House
- 1825 The remodelling of Buckingham House by John Nash begins
- 1847–50 Fourth side of the palace built
- 1851 Marble Arch is moved to Park Lane
- 1902 Edward VII begins a major redecoration project
- 1940 The chapel is bombed on 13 September
- 1993 The State Rooms are opened to the public for the first time
- 2002 Queen Elizabeth II's Golden Jubilee celebrations take place in June

Buckingham Palace is one of the most famous royal palaces in the world. Its familiarity has increased since the advent of television, as it is the focal point of most major royal events, such as weddings and other ceremonial occasions. Each day, hundreds of tourists gather outside the wrought-iron gates of the palace to watch the Changing of the Guard and each summer the Queen holds a series of parties in the extensive gardens at the rear of the palace. In addition, there are usually 20 investitures each year at Buckingham Palace, in which honours are conferred on celebrities as well as people who are less well known. Such events, however, are merely the tip of a very large iceberg, as Buckingham Palace is a working palace that employs 450 people. The business of state is conducted here, with the Queen and the Duke of Edinburgh receiving many guests in both formal and informal settings. The Royal Standard flutters from the flagpole when the Queen is in residence, but it is always business as usual whether she is there or not.

Buckingham House

The first building to stand on the spot that is now occupied by Buckingham Palace was Goring House, erected in 1633 by Lord Goring. It was a country house on what was then a border of London, surrounded by the greenery of St James's Park and Hyde Park. After a disastrous fire in 1675, it was rebuilt in 1677 as

▶ *The Grand Staircase was designed by John Nash for George IV and leads up to the State Rooms on the first floor of the palace.*

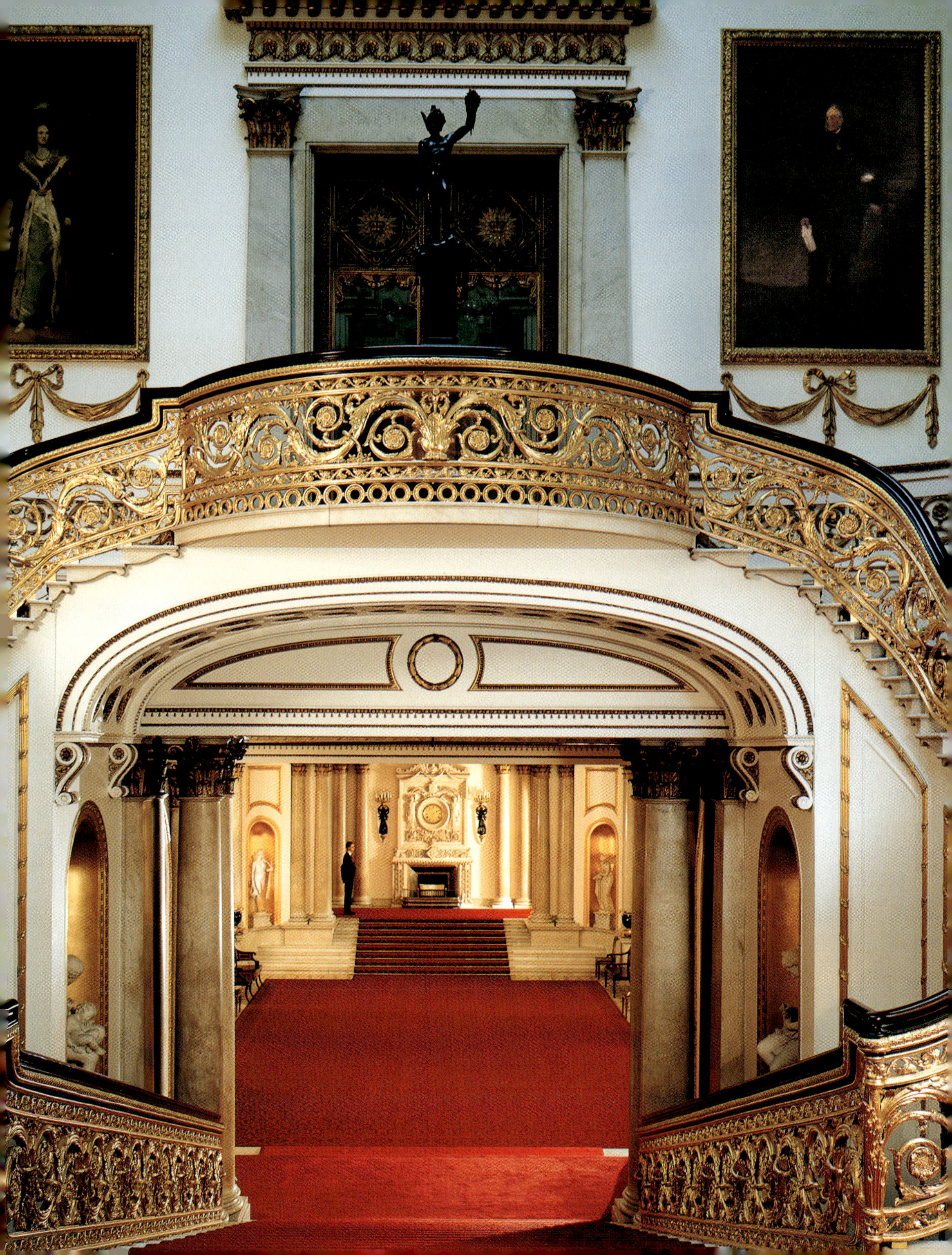

Arlington House, and once again in 1702–5 as Buckingham House, when it was named for its owner, the 1st Duke of Buckingham. When the duke died in 1721, his widow failed in her attempt to sell the property to the Prince of Wales, who later became George II, but eventually the duke's son sold Buckingham House to George III in 1761 for £28,000. George III and his wife, Queen Charlotte, used it as their family home, while the ceremonial life of the court continued to be conducted at St James's Palace. Buckingham House was gradually extended, but by the time the Prince Regent had acquired it, after the death of his mother in 1818, he knew it was not big enough to suit his needs.

The Prince Regent

At the time, the Prince Regent had nearly finished the creation of the Royal Pavilion, in Brighton, and Carlton House, which lay at the opposite end of the Mall to Buckingham House. He had filled Carlton House with the finest examples of French furniture, which had recently come on to

INTERESTING FEATURES

- The Grand Staircase
- The Grand Hall
- The Nash ceiling of the Green Drawing Room
- The Throne Room
- The Picture Gallery
- The organ in the Ballroom, which was taken from the Royal Pavilion
- Portraits of Hanoverian sovereigns in the State Dining Room
- The Table of the Grand Commanders in the Blue Drawing Room

the market after the end of the French Revolution; all of these are in the Royal Collection today. The Prince Regent had lavished massive amounts of money on Carlton House, but by 1815 he was finding it too small for his needs.

Funding the project

The Prince Regent's acquisition of Buckingham House set alarm bells ringing in Parliament. His previous building projects had run massively over budget and the country was in straitened circumstances after the enormous expenses of the Napoleonic Wars. In 1819, Parliament gave him £150,000 to develop Buckingham Palace, which fell far short of the £450,000 demanded by the prince. He was told that Crown property would have to be sold to

The east front of Buckingham Palace was a late addition that was built to create more living space for Queen Victoria and Prince Albert.

raise additional funds, so in 1825 Carlton House was demolished and the land developed (Carlton House Terrace now stands on the site).

From a private home to a palace

When George III died in 1820, the Prince Regent became George IV. In 1821, he commissioned John Nash to start redesigning Buckingham House. The original plan was to enlarge the existing building to create a private house for the king. Work began on this in 1825 by extending the shell of Buckingham House and building a smaller wing at right angles on either side of it. However, as with so many of George IV's ideas, this original plan was no sooner completed than it was eclipsed by his much more elaborate and opulent scheme to create a proper palace. Pity John Nash, who had already fulfilled his brief to build a private home for the king

BUCKINGHAM PALACE

and who was now caught between Parliament, who held the purse strings, and George IV, who believed that he had the right to whatever he wanted. Nash created the desired palace by raising the height of the two wings. In 1827, the empty fourth side of the square contained what we know now as Marble Arch, which was modelled on the Arch of Constantine in Rome and formed the main entrance to the palace. It was moved to its present position at the top of Park Lane in 1851.

George IV died in 1830 and, following a parliamentary inquiry in 1831, Nash was sacked for 'inexcusable irregularity and gross negligence'. Despite the lavish amounts of money that had been spent on the palace, it was not yet finished. George IV's younger brother, William IV, became king and the architect Edward Blore, fresh from designing Lambeth Palace, was commissioned to continue the work, but on a far less grand and extravagant scale.

Victoria and Albert
It soon became obvious that Buckingham Palace lacked the number of rooms needed for staff if it was to operate as a fully functioning palace. To remedy this, Blore built new offices in the south wing and added another storey to the main block. When the Houses of Parliament burned down in October 1834, William IV made the hopeful suggestion that Parliament should move into Buckingham Palace, which he heartily disliked. Much to his disappointment it was decided to rebuild the Houses of Parliament and keep Buckingham Palace as a royal residence. William IV never actually lived at Buckingham Palace, as it was still partly unfinished when he died in 1837. When his young niece, Victoria, inherited the throne, she moved in almost immediately, only to find that many of the windows would not open and there was something very wrong with the drains. By the time Victoria married Prince Albert of Saxe-Coburg and Gotha in 1840 and started a family, the palace still lacked enough rooms to be a family home. The cheapest solution to this was to move Marble Arch to its present position and build an eastern range to the U-shaped palace, thus creating a four-sided palace surrounding a central quadrangle. This work was designed by Edward Blore and carried out by Thomas Cubitt between 1847 and 1850.

Income tax was about to be introduced on a permanent basis and no one wanted to be accused of financing royal extravagance at the expense of its subjects. Agreeing to sell the Royal Pavilion to Brighton council in 1846 raised some money and, as it was believed that the Pavilion would be demolished, its contents were removed and initially stored at Kensington Palace. Many items were later used to furnish some of the rooms at Buckingham Palace, much to Blore's horror, as he considered them to be far too fussy. In the early 1850s, a new southwest block was built to create a massive ballroom with kitchens below.

Life at the palace continued happily for Victoria and Albert, with all but one of their children being born here. Tragedy struck, however, on 14 December 1861, when Prince Albert died of typhoid fever at Windsor Castle. His devastated widow retired into deep mourning at Windsor Castle and Osborne House, and Buckingham Palace was virtually mothballed for decades. It was occasionally used for state occasions and family gatherings, but

▼ *The semi-tented ceiling in the White Drawing Room was designed by John Nash and has survived the renovations that were made to the room in the late 19th century.*

for the most part it remained ignored. The palace had a brief renaissance during Victoria's Golden Jubilee celebrations in 1887, but once the festivities were over it returned to its shuttered state.

A 'ritzy' makeover

Such neglect and disuse meant that Edward VII inherited a very old-fashioned and musty palace when he succeeded to the throne on 22 January 1901. The old century had died, and with it Victoria, so her son wanted to breathe some fresh, 20th-century life into his London palace. He appointed Frank T. Verity as architect and C. H. Besant as designer. Unfortunately, many of their decorative flourishes, which involved a great deal of white paint and elaborate gilding, were completely out of sympathy with Nash's original designs. These additions can still be seen today in the Grand Staircase, Marble Hall, Ballroom and Grand Entrance. If some of these rooms bear a strong resemblance to early 20th-century grand hotels such as the Ritz or the Savoy, it is because Edward VII liked things to look 'ritzy'. Of course, these Edwardian decorations reflected the tastes of their time, just as Nash's designs reflected the tastes of the Regency period.

New façade

These Edwardian changes cut little ice with Queen Mary, who lived at Buckingham Palace with her husband, George V, between 1910 and 1936. She took a great interest in the contents of all the royal palaces, and worked hard to recapture some of the Regency flavour that had been lost during successive improvements at Buckingham Palace. Shortly after the start of her reign, the Caen stone on the east front of the palace began to disintegrate because of the polluted London air. The entire front was redesigned and then resurfaced in Portland stone, to make it look more fitting as the principal palace of the royal family. Sir Aston Webb was commissioned to design the new frontage, and he was also responsible for the design of the Queen Victoria Memorial, which was erected in front of the palace in 1911.

The Second World War

Not every royal inhabitant of the palace had treasured memories of it. Edward VIII, who on his abdication in 1936 became the Duke of Windsor, declared in his memoirs: 'The vast building with its stately rooms and endless corridors and passages, seemed pervaded by a curious, musty smell that still assails me. I was never happy there.'

Fortunately, his successor, George VI, had much warmer memories of their shared childhood in the palace. His reign had barely begun when the Second World War broke out, and the palace became an important focal point for national morale. George VI conducted target practice in the garden, much to the alarm of passing courtiers. When it was too dangerous to sleep in

London because of the bombing raids, the king and queen would spend each night at Windsor Castle and return to Buckingham Palace early the following morning to give the nation a sense of continuity and solidarity. Their two daughters, the Princesses Elizabeth and Margaret, spent most of the war at Windsor Castle.

One of the most memorable events in the palace's modern history took place on VE Day, 8 May 1945, when the country celebrated Germany's unconditional surrender the previous day. London's streets, illuminated after over five years of enforced blackouts, were crowded with people who converged on the palace and waited cheerfully for the royal family and the Prime Minister, Winston Churchill, to appear on the balcony. After a final curtain call, George VI asked some young officers to smuggle Princesses Elizabeth and Margaret out of the palace to mingle anonymously with the crowds and enjoy the atmosphere.

Royal wedding

Another world-famous event took place at the palace on 29 July 1981, when Prince Charles married Lady Diana Spencer. This royal wedding captured the world's imagination. The Mall was lined with international camera crews, who were quickly joined by thousands of sightseers, and all eyes were trained on the balcony. As always on such occasions, there are often tantalizing glimpses of the room that lies behind the balcony. This room is known as the Centre Room, and has three floor-to-ceiling windows that open onto the balcony with its commanding view of the Queen Victoria Memorial and the length of the Mall stretching beyond it. The room has strong overtones of the Royal Pavilion, with a central gasolier that would not look out of place there and yellow Chinese wallpaper that was probably originally intended for the Pavilion. George IV died before Buckingham Palace was fit to live in, but how he would have enjoyed standing on the balcony in all his finery, waving to his cheering subjects.

information

Contact details

Buckingham Palace
London
SW1A 1AA

+44 (0)20 7766 7300

Official website of the Royal Monarchy, Buckingham Palace site includes a virtual tour
www.royal.gov.uk/TheRoyal Residences/BuckinghamPalace /BuckinghamPalace.aspx

Transport links

Victoria

Victoria, Green Park, St James's Park or Hyde Park Corner

THE TOWER OF LONDON
London

KEY DATES

✠ *1100 The White Tower is completed*

✠ *c.1240 The Salt Tower built*

✠ *1471 Henry VI murdered in the Tower on 21 May*

✠ *1483 Edward V and Prince Richard murdered in the Tower*

✠ *1642–9 Tower controlled by the Parliamentarians*

✠ *1671 An attempt by Colonel Blood to steal the Crown Jewels*

✠ *1810 Removal of the Royal Mint*

✠ *1841 The Grand Storehouse burns down in October*

✠ *1914–6 Eleven spies held in the Tower*

✠ *1941 Rudolf Hess held in the Queen's House for four days in May*

In its time, the Tower of London has been a fortress, a royal palace, a prison, a place of execution for those of noble birth, a zoo, a mint, an armoury, the repository of the Crown Jewels and a major tourist attraction. William I originally built it, soon after the Battle of Hastings, in order to establish a secure, defensive London base in a country where the Norman Conquest was profoundly unpopular. It was not the only fortress to be built in London by the Normans: they also built castles in the areas we now know as Blackfriars and Ludgate Circus, among others.

Norman building

When you visit the Tower today and see a large complex of buildings neatly contained within an outer wall, it is natural to assume that it was originally built this way. What you actually see is a mixture of original walls and buildings, and those that were created specifically for the Tower over the centuries. What initially attracted the Normans to the site was the strong city wall that already bordered the River Thames on two sides. The wall was built by the Romans during their occupation of Britain between AD 43 and 410. The Normans dug a ditch along the two unwalled sides and secured it with a timber enclosure to create a roughly rectangular plot, within which they began to build. They built the massive White Tower as a fortified palace. It was a watershed in architectural history as it is believed to be the earliest

▶ *The medieval kings of England lived with their families and royal court in the White Tower, as it was then the seat of government.*

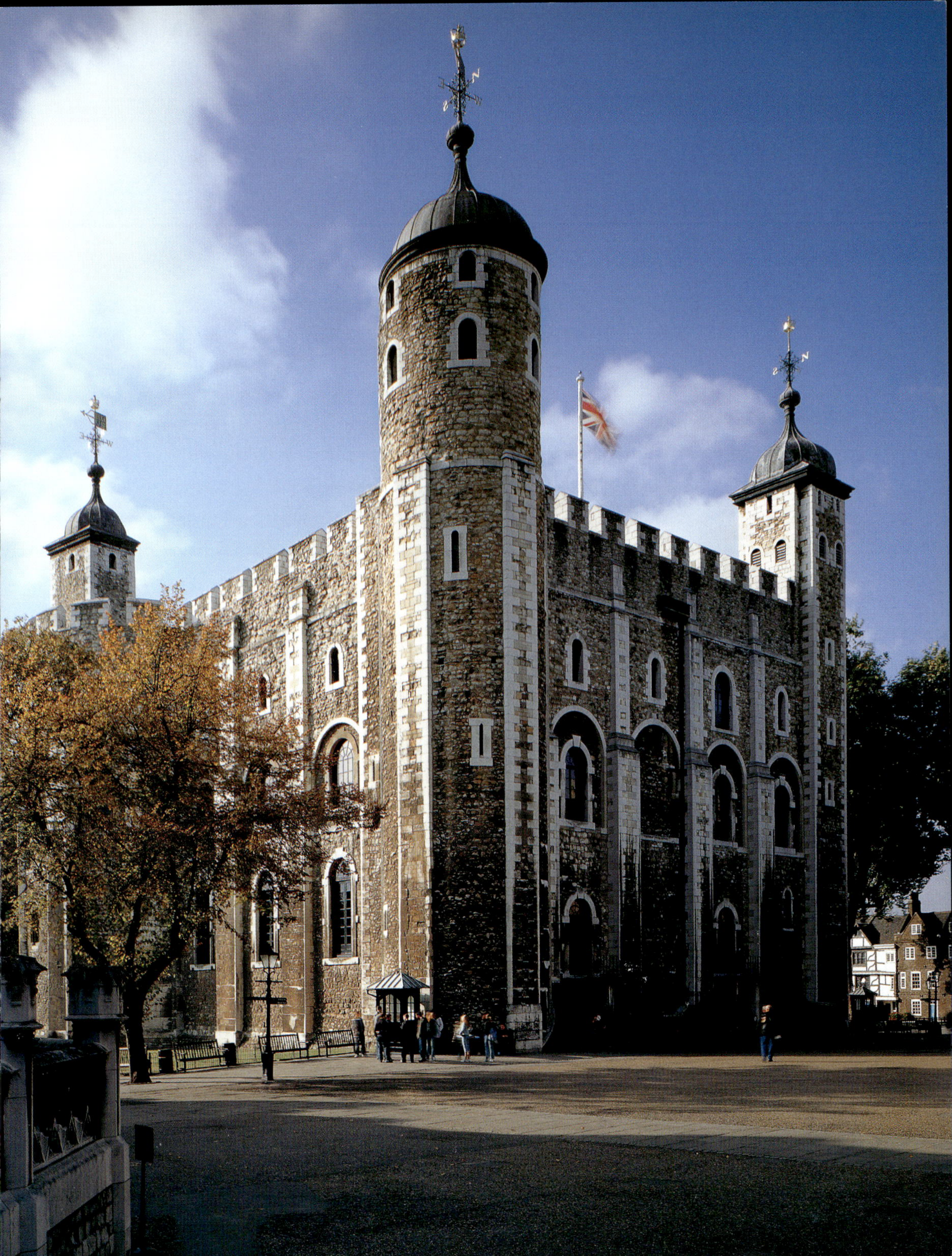

building in Britain to have fireplaces built into the walls. Another innovation was latrines built into the outer walls. As the White Tower was a royal palace, it needed a chapel, so the Chapel Royal of St John the Evangelist, a beautiful example of Romanesque architecture, was built. It is now the oldest Norman church in the country and it is believed that the now plain walls were originally painted.

Defensive structures

The death of William the Conqueror in 1087 left the White Tower unfinished, but it was completed during the reign of his son, William Rufus. Successive kings carried out more work on the White Tower and were also instrumental in building other towers such as the Wardrobe and Bell Towers. However, it was not until the 13th and 14th centuries that the Tower of London was given the inner curtain wall – the outer wall and the moat that we know today.

The Tower becomes uninhabitable

The last sovereign to use the Tower as a royal palace was James I, who followed a time-honoured tradition by staying at the Tower before his coronation in 1604. By this time it was in a sorry state: some of the

▼ *The White Tower, dating from the time of William the Conqueror, stands at the centre of a complex of towers, armouries, barracks, fortifications and the dry moat that make up the Tower of London.*

> ## INTERESTING FEATURES
>
> - ✠ The White Tower
> - ✠ The Chapel of St John the Evangelist
> - ✠ Traitors' Gate
> - ✠ The upper chamber of the Wakefield Tower
> - ✠ The oratory in St Thomas's Tower
> - ✠ The wall walk
> - ✠ The Crown Jewels
> - ✠ The Bloody Tower
> - ✠ The Queen's House
> - ✠ The execution site on Tower Green
> - ✠ The Chapel Royal of St Peter ad Vincula

roofs had collapsed and had to be repaired in a makeshift fashion. Although James had insisted on being shown around the many buildings, the place was no longer habitable. By the time of the coronation of Charles II in April 1661, the Tower's condition had deteriorated to such an extent that he was unable to stay there. Anxious to keep up with tradition, however, the royal procession rode to the gates of the Tower at dawn on the day of the coronation in order to at least start the parade from there.

The Royal Menagerie

For exactly 600 years, from 1235 to 1835, the Tower was home to the Royal Menagerie. For most of this time the collection consisted of royal gifts; animals were only bought for the menagerie after 1822. The menagerie began in 1235 with three leopards, given to Henry III by Frederick II, the Holy Roman Emperor. The choice of creatures acknowledged the three leopards adorning the coat of arms of the House of Plantagenet, to which Henry belonged. Sixteen years later, a polar bear arrived from Norway; the Sheriffs of London had to pay 4d a day for its food. The bear was allowed to fish in the Thames, although it was kept secure with an iron chain. Incredibly, in 1255, Henry's cousin, Louis IX of France, gave him an elephant; an elephant house was built to accommodate the creature and it even had its own keeper. It is believed to be the first elephant ever seen in England. It was buried within the grounds of the Tower.

The collection of animals grew steadily over the years as more creatures were given to the king or queen of the time.

The menagerie was opened to the public during Elizabeth I's reign, and proved very popular until the 1830s when, for a combination of commercial and animal welfare reasons, the royal collection was given to the Zoological Society of London, which had recently established a new zoo in Regent's Park. This is now London Zoo, one of the biggest zoos in the world.

Involuntary guests
Other parts of the Tower were also opened to the public during the reign of Elizabeth I, and proved to be an enjoyable day out for most. However, many of the Tower's involuntary visitors had a very different experience of the place. In addition to its many other roles, the Tower was, after all, a prison and fortress housing royal prisoners as well as commoners who had displeased the Crown. The Welsh Prince of Wales, Llywelyn ap Gruffydd, was a captive here from 1241–4. He fell to his death while trying to escape.

During the Wars of the Roses, the deposed Henry VI was imprisoned in the Tower in 1461 and 1470, and again in 1471; during these times the Yorkist Edward IV occupied the throne. Henry died in the Tower on 21 May 1471; it is believed that he was murdered, probably on the orders of Edward IV, while praying in the tiny chapel in the Wakefield Tower. Legend has it that his murderer was Edward's brother, the

This view of the Tower of London was taken from Tower Hill in the early 1900s. The moat is just visible behind the trunks of the trees.

Duke of Gloucester, who later became Richard III. Another notorious chapter in English history involves Richard and his two nephews, the 'Princes in the Tower'.

The Princes in the Tower

After the death of Edward IV in April 1483, the throne passed to his 12-year-old son, Edward V. Richard was appointed Protector of his young nephew, and placed him and his younger brother in the Tower for alleged safekeeping. Richard then had both boys declared illegitimate on the grounds that their father's marriage was invalid. As a result of this, Parliament invited Richard to take the throne and he was crowned that July; by then, the two princes had not been seen in the Tower for a month. It was widely believed that Richard had murdered them, and he was publicly reviled. Historians have debated the merits of the case ever since. Although popular legend has it that the princes were murdered in the suitably named Bloody Tower, it is more likely that they died in the White Tower. In 1674, the skeletons of two children were discovered during the demolition of a 12th-century building attached to the White Tower. They were identified as belonging to the two princes and buried in Westminster Abbey in 1678 on the orders of Charles II.

The Bloody Tower

Over the centuries, since being built in the early 1220s, a wealth of legends and grisly tales has accumulated about the Bloody Tower. It originally went under the much happier name of the Garden Tower, but earned its present name during Tudor times because of the widespread belief that it was where the Princes in the Tower had died. The upper part of the tower was altered in

The first-floor room in the Wakefield Tower is a reconstruction of how it would have looked in the 13th century.

THE TOWER OF LONDON 77

about 1360, and again in 1603, when it was heightened and an extra floor was added to provide more accommodation for Sir Walter Raleigh and his family. Raleigh was imprisoned here from 1603–16 for plotting against James I, and his family were allowed to live here with him; this was common practice for important prisoners, who lived here in some comfort.

Sometimes prisoners were confined to the Tower by members of their own families. This was an experience shared by both Anne Boleyn in 1536 and, in 1554, by her daughter, Princess Elizabeth. Anne was sent there on the orders of her husband, Henry VIII, who had grown tired of her and was increasingly desperate to find a wife who could give him a son and therefore ensure the succession. Elizabeth was confined in the Tower on the orders of her half-sister, Mary I, who wrongly believed that Elizabeth had taken part in

▼ *The Queen's House, built in 1540 for the king's representative at the Tower, is now the home of the Tower's resident governor. It is the only 16th-century building to survive within the Tower's precincts.*

a rebellion against her marriage to Philip II of Spain. Elizabeth had the good fortune to be released from the Tower, but Anne was executed on Tower Green in May 1536.

Traitors' Gate

Both Anne and Elizabeth entered the Tower through Traitors' Gate, a low gateway in St Thomas's Tower that was originally designed in the 1270s for Edward I to use as a water gate. It became known as Traitors' Gate because prisoners who were accused of treason entered the Tower through it; for most of the prisoners, it was a one-way trip into the Tower of London. Traitors' Gate can still be seen today, and it is easy to imagine the dread with which prisoners passed through it. The timber buildings above it date it from the early 1530s.

Executions at the Tower

Most prisoners of the Tower who were here under sentence of death were executed in public on Tower Hill, just outside the Tower's walls, where overexcited and noisy crowds would gather to watch the proceedings. However, seven prisoners were beheaded on Tower Green, within the Tower's precincts, to avoid the chaos that would have ensued if any of these events had taken place in public. Two of Henry VIII's wives were dispatched here: his second wife, Anne Boleyn, who was beheaded with a sword instead of the customary axe and was the first English queen to be publicly executed; and his fifth wife, Catherine Howard, who was executed in 1542. Lady Jane Grey, a hapless pawn of her ambitious father-in-law in a plot to ensure the Protestant succession, was beheaded on Tower Green on 12 February 1554. She had been proclaimed queen of England on 10 July 1553 following the death of Edward VI four days earlier, and ruled for nine days before Mary I claimed the throne and had Lady Jane imprisoned.

The Chapel Royal

The bodies of all seven royal prisoners, as well as those of many other prisoners who died in the Tower, were all buried in the Chapel Royal of St Peter ad Vincula, which stands behind Tower Green. The name of the chapel means 'St Peter in chains', and it was built in the 12th century for the use of prisoners of the Tower. At that time, it stood apart from the Tower, and only became incorporated within its walls during the 13th century when Henry III decided to have the Tower enlarged. The chapel has been rebuilt twice since that time: firstly during the reign of Edward I, and once again in 1519–20. The chapel was restored in 1876 when it was discovered that the bodies of the beheaded prisoners had been buried under the nave and chancel in a rather random and higgledy-piggledy fashion. They were dug up and reinterred beneath the marble pavement that lies in front of the altar.

The Crown Jewels

One of the biggest attractions at the Tower of London is the display of the Crown Jewels, which are guarded by the Yeoman Warders in the Jewel Tower. They have been kept on public display since the 17th century. Most of the treasures on show are known as the 'coronation regalia'; as their name implies, they are used at coronations. They include the sovereign's orb and sceptre, which were made for the coronation of Charles II after the restoration of the monarchy in 1660. In fact, most of the coronation regalia dates from this time as it replaced all the regalia that was melted down after the execution of Charles I. There are also rings, swords, spurs,

▼ *The Chapel Royal of St Peter ad Vincula is the oldest Chapel Royal in England. It was defined by Henry VIII as the parish church of the Tower.*

bracelets and robes on display, all of which still play a role in the English coronation.

Not surprisingly, security has not always been as tight as it is today. In 1671 there was an audacious and almost successful attempt by Colonel Thomas Blood to steal the Crown Jewels in the Jewel House. Blood first disguised himself as a clergyman and went with his nephew to the Jewel House, where they started chatting to the keeper. They were invited to supper, during which time they admired the keeper's pistols, which he duly sold to them. This was a very clever ruse because it left him unarmed. The following morning, Blood and some friends arrived to view the jewels and easily managed to overpower the keeper. They were busily stealing the jewels when they were disturbed and had to escape. Members of the Tower's garrison caught them all carrying items of regalia; Colonel Blood had flattened the crown with a mallet and stuffed it in a bag. Blood insisted upon speaking only to Charles II, who was so charmed that, rather than punish him, he fully pardoned him and even gave him estates in Ireland and an annual pension.

Tourism

Today, the Tower is still a thriving hub of activity, thanks to the countless tourists who stream through its gates each year. The red-coated Yeomen Warders, affectionately known as Beefeaters, give vivid guided tours in addition to their military duties. Each evening, the Tower reverts to its role as a fortress during the Ceremony of the Keys, in which the outer gates of the Tower are locked and ceremoniously handed over to the resident governor of the Tower. It is an impressive reminder that, despite the Tower's role as one of the main tourist attractions in Britain, it is still a fortress that must be protected.

information

Contact details

Tower Hill
London
EC3N 4AB

0844 482 7777 (from the UK)
+44 (0)20 3166 6000 (from outside the UK)

Historic Royal Palaces site
www.hrp.org.uk/TowerOfLondon

Transport links

Fenchurch Street (exit Mark Lane; turn left on Byward Street to Tower Hill); London Bridge (15-minute walk). Also Docklands Light Railway (DLR) to Tower Gateway station (located adjacent to Tower Hill tube station

15, 42, 78, 100, RV1; also all major sightseeing bus tours

Tower Pier (from Charing Cross, Westminster and Greenwich)

Tower Hill (5 minute walk, signposted)

There are three bicycle stands at the Tower located next to the main shop

SOMERSET HOUSE
London

KEY DATES

✠ *1547* Edward Seymour begins to build his great palace

✠ *1553* The palace is finished and passes to the Princess Elizabeth

✠ *1603* The palace is given to Anne of Denmark and Norway and renamed Denmark House

✠ *1609* Inigo Jones undertakes substantial renovations

✠ *1619* Anne dies and the house passes to Henrietta Maria

✠ *1630* The Queen's Chapel is completed

✠ *1658* Oliver Cromwell's body lies in state in the palace

✠ *1685* Catherine of Braganza takes up residence there; she is the last queen to live there

✠ *1775* The original Somerset House is demolished; a new building is erected in its stead

Somerset House was once the site of a beautiful Tudor palace. Today it is famous as the neoclassical building situated between the Strand and the River Thames and for its open-air concerts and the films shown there during the summer months and the ice rink in the winter.

The Lord Protector

By the 16th century, the Strand's river frontage was a popular place for the rich and influential to build their residences – bishops, such as those of Exeter, Bath and Wells, and Norwich and Durham, the dukes of Richmond, Norfolk and Suffolk, and the king and queen were among the people who owned houses there. Many members of the aristocracy similarly aspired to do so, including Edward Seymour.

Seymour had arguably become the most important man in England. Following Henry VIII's death, Seymour was made the Duke of Somerset and the Lord Protector of Henry's very young son Edward VI until the young king reached his majority. In 1547, Seymour began to plan his new palace on the site of land he already owned, on a key thoroughfare between the Tower of London to the east and the Palace of Westminster to the west. However, this involved the demolition of several chapels and churches, a move that was particularly controversial and resulted in Seymour's imprisonment in the Tower of London in 1549, albeit briefly.

▲ *From the late 1300s, the Strand area and riverside was a popular place to reside, particularly for those who sought influence at Westminster.*

A palace fit for a king or queen

By 1551, Seymour's palace was almost complete, but he had little opportunity to enjoy it as he was again arrested, this time on the charge of treason. He was executed in January 1552. As for the palace, it is thought that either John of Padua or John Thynne acted as the architect. The resulting courtyard house cost about £10,000 to build. The Strand façade was obviously influenced by classical traditions, combining both Doric and Ionic pillars. It had a gatehouse to the Strand and a great hall sat opposite the riverfront.

With Seymour gone, the palace now passed to the Crown. After it was finally finished in 1553, it was given to the young Princess Elizabeth (the future Elizabeth I). Over the years, it was largely used for meetings of her council and as a lodging house for foreign diplomats, as she preferred St James's or Whitehall when in London.

Denmark House

Following Elizabeth I's death in 1603, the palace passed to the new Stuart King James I (James VI of Scotland). He gave it to his wife Anne of Denmark for her private use. Anne proceeded to turn what by now was known as 'Denmark House' into an artistic and social centre of court life. She held extravagant masques at the house, commissioning playwrights such as Ben Jonson to write and Inigo Jones to design sets. It was Jones who largely undertook the substantial redesign of Denmark House after 1609 with building works that cost more than £34,000, which made it one of the most expensive buildings of that time.

The original lower court was remodelled and a new three-sided courtyard was erected. An open arcade, featuring nine arches, was added to the entrance and the ranges on the east and west were rebuilt to match the original Strand front. The riverfront was rendered in imitation stone and the paintwork, gilding and redecoration were unfinished when Anne died in 1619.

Inigo Jones' reign continues

Even after Anne's death, work continued on the building and was overseen by Jones, aided by John Webb and Nicholas Stone. By this time Charles I was on the throne with his queen, Henrietta Maria. The new queen's chapel, which was finished in 1630, was the most impressive addition to the place but it was for Catholic mass and helped fuel the fires already raging against the king, which would lead to his demise. In addition to the chapel, Jones improved Denmark House by building, among other things, a cistern house, an arbour and a beautifully decorated cabinet room. Henrietta Maria lived there until she was forced to flee to France, just before Charles I's execution.

Somerset House is today a popular open-air venue for live music and other events in the summer – and also houses an open-air ice rink.

Civil War and the Restoration

During the Civil War, the house was largely used as the headquarters for General Fairfax, the Parliamentary commander-in-chief. When Oliver Cromwell died in 1658, his body lay in state at Somerset House. Much of the royal collection of art was also gathered there in 1659 before being sold to aid the army.

In 1660, Charles II was restored to the throne of England and his mother, now the dowager queen, came to live at the house again. During this time more work was done – as well as a stables and a new building to house the presence chamber and privy chamber, a riverside gallery was constructed. It served as the model for the Strand front of the modern Somerset House with its five open arches.

Henrietta Maria left England as the plague reached its height in London in 1665 and never returned. The house was left to Charles II's wife, Catherine of Braganza, who began major works on it. After her husband's death, Catherine took up permanent residence there and Christopher Wren began redecorating the house from 1685. Catherine was the last queen to live at the palace. She left England in 1693 to become Regent of Portugal.

The final years

In the 18th century Somerset House was increasingly neglected. Used for a variety of purposes, including storage and providing lodgings for foreign dignatories, by 1718 Vanbrugh commented that the building was in a sad state, the worst of all the royal palaces. Four years later, the Horse Guards took over the stables and from 1756 foot soldiers were stationed there. As the house fell into ruin, George III made the sad decision to pull it down and Buckingham Palace became the dower house of the queen. In 1775 demolition work began and the new building was erected around it and finished in 1786.

information

Contact details

Somerset House Trust
South Building
Somerset House
Strand London WC2R 1LA

+44 (0)20 7845 4600

Somerset House
www.somersethouse.org.uk

Transport links

Charing Cross, Waterloo and Blackfriars

6, 9, 11, 13, 15, 23, 77a, 91 and 176

River Bus: Embankment and Savoy piers

KENSINGTON PALACE
London

KEY DATES

- 1689 William III and Mary II buy Nottingham House
- 1689 First phase of building work
- 1690–2 Second phase of building work
- 1691 Fire destroys part of the south range of the Great Court in November
- 1695 Third phase of building work
- 1689 Sir Christopher Wren builds the Grand Staircase
- 1718–27 Fourth phase of building work
- 1722–7 William Kent paints the ceilings
- 1807–11 New apartments created for the Duke of Kent
- 1819 Princess Victoria born at the palace on 24 May
- 1911–76 State apartments occupied by the London Museum
- 1981–97 Diana, Princess of Wales, lives at the palace

Not far from the roaring traffic of High Street Kensington in London, amid the greenery of Kensington Gardens, is a 17th-century royal palace. In its time it has been home to several reigning monarchs: William III and Mary II, Queen Anne, George I and George II. It was also the birthplace and home of Princess Victoria, who became queen in 1837. Kensington Palace is still home to some members of the royal family; in recent years the most notable residents have been Princess Margaret and Princess Diana.

A private house for William and Mary

William III and Mary II were responsible for the building of Kensington Palace in the 1690s. Both Protestants, they had been invited to take over the British throne in 1688 when the Catholic sympathies of Mary's father, James II, were making him increasingly unpopular. They duly arrived from the Netherlands and James fled to France, allegedly running over Westminster Bridge in such a hurry that he accidentally dropped the Great Seal in the River Thames.

The new king and queen had not long been established in England before William's delicate health began to suffer at Whitehall Palace, which was then the official London residence of the royal family. Whitehall was very close to the River Thames, which meant that those living there had to endure the appalling stench that arose from it, especially in the summer: raw sewage

▶ *The south front of the palace was built in 1695. It was the final addition to the palace made during the reign of William III.*

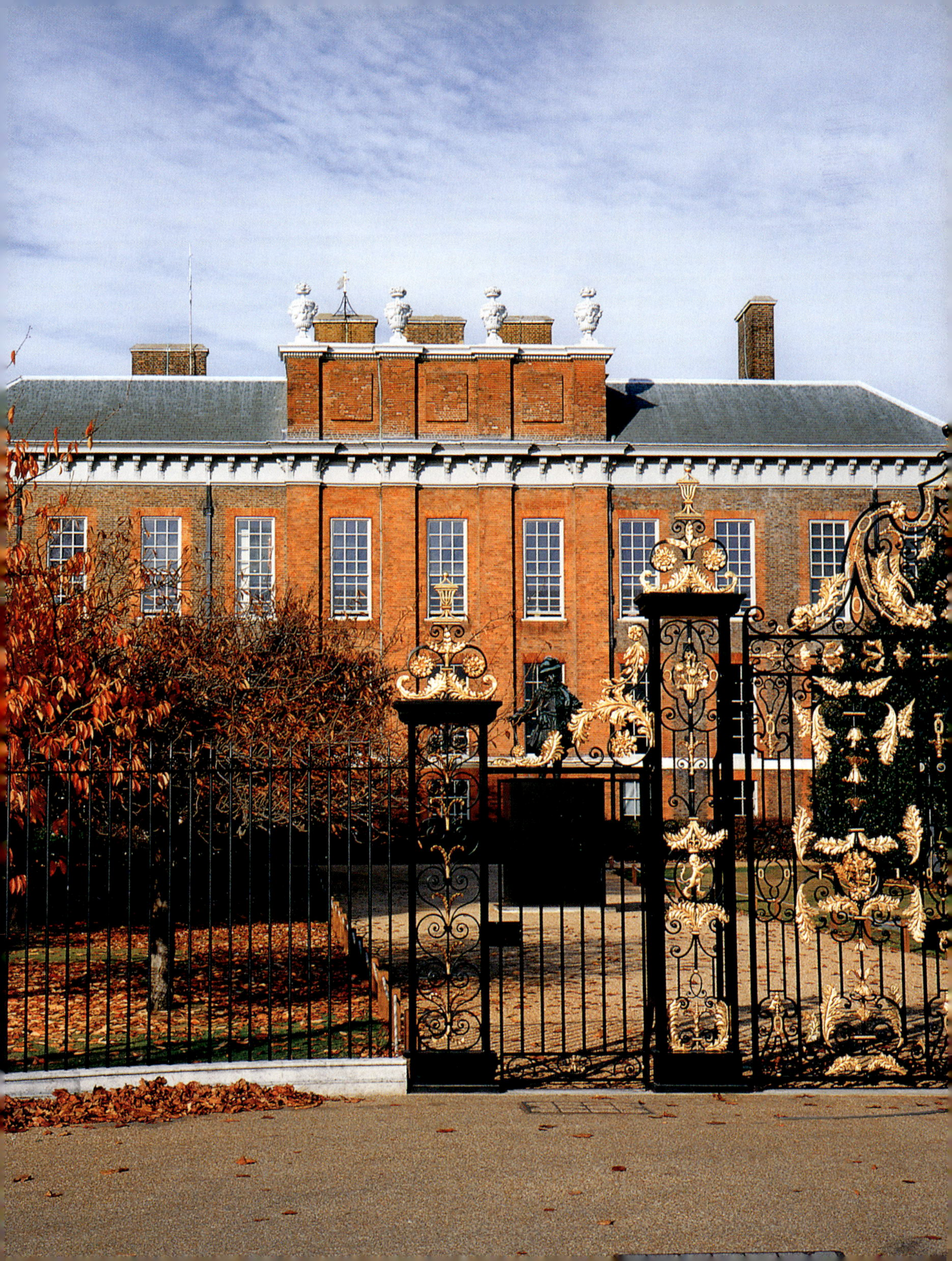

INTERESTING FEATURES

- ✠ The King's Grand Staircase
- ✠ The Presence Chamber
- ✠ The Cupola Room
- ✠ Queen Victoria's bedroom
- ✠ The King's Gallery
- ✠ Queen Mary's dining room
- ✠ Queen Mary's bedchamber
- ✠ The sunken garden

flowed straight into it, as it did into every other London river.

Renovations had already started on Hampton Court, but William and Mary also needed a private London home to stay in each winter to be near the government in Westminster; Parliament did not sit in the summer because of the smell of the River Thames. They found the ideal property in Kensington: Nottingham House, a Jacobean mansion built around 1605, for which they paid £20,000. Work on the house started at once and was overseen by Sir Christopher Wren. A three-storey pavilion was built onto each corner of the original house and a wing was added for courtiers. William and Mary proved to be impatient new owners, as they moved in only a few months after buying the house even though building work was still going on.

A second phase of improvements was carried out between 1690 and 1692. At this point, the building was known as Kensington House to reiterate the point that it was a private home rather than an official palace. Mary was not able to enjoy her royal retreat for long and died of smallpox there on 28 December 1694. William instigated the next phase of improvements in 1695, before dying at the palace on 8 March 1702.

The Orangery

William's successor, Queen Anne, also made her mark on the site. She was particularly interested in the gardens, and had the Orangery built. Designed by Nicholas Hawksmoor and Sir John Vanbrugh, the Orangery housed tender plants in the winter and was used for court entertainments in the summer, when the plants could be safely left outside. Today, the Orangery is a restaurant for visitors.

Although Queen Anne conceived 19 children and had five live births, none of her

▶ *The King's Gallery was built for William III in 1695. He died at Kensington Palace five days after a riding accident at Hampton Court in 1702.*

88 LONDON

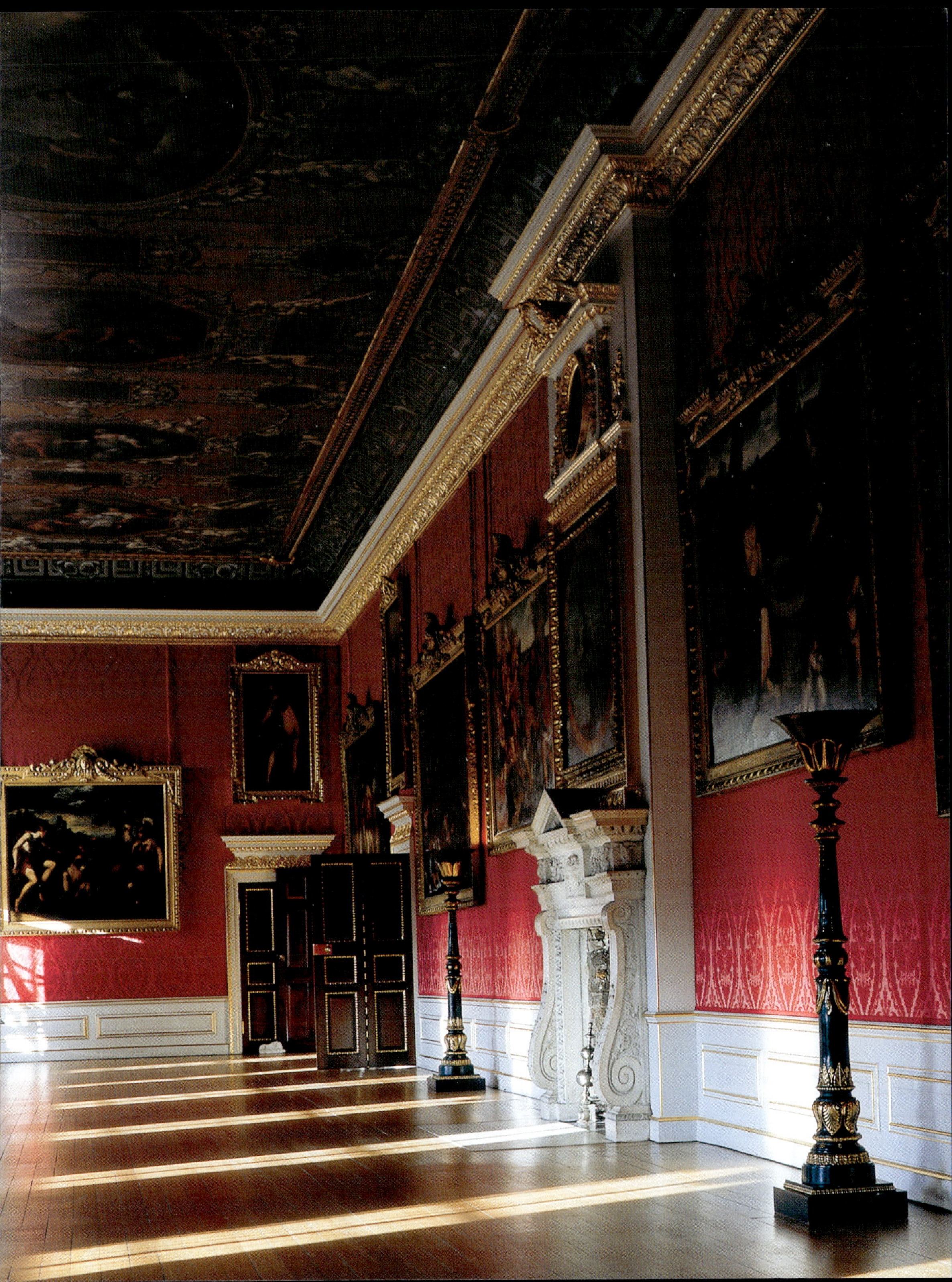

90 LONDON

children outlived her, so when she died at the palace on 1 August 1714 the succession passed to her third cousin, Prince George of Hanover. Anne's death marked the end of the House of Stuart and the beginning of the reign of the House of Hanover. George I inherited the British throne through his mother, Sophia, who was a Protestant granddaughter of James I. In preparation for his eventual succession, he had already become a naturalized British subject in 1705. When George I arrived in Britain, Kensington Palace became his London home. He instigated a new round of building and was responsible for the creation of the Cupola Room, the Privy Chamber and the Withdrawing Room. In total, so much work was carried out under George's instructions that he was never able to make full use of the palace; the place was habitually overrun with builders carrying out his orders.

His son, George II, was the last reigning monarch to live at Kensington Palace. He was very conscious of the unpopularity of the new Hanoverian kings and wanted to underline his English nationality. Before addressing Parliament for the first time after he became George II in 1727, he felt compelled to announce in his heavy German accent: 'I have not a drop of blood in my veins which is not English.'

◄ *The Cupola Room was the setting for the christening of Victoria (the future Queen Victoria), daughter of the Duke and Duchess of Kent.*

On average, George II spent a good part of each year at the palace, although large areas of it were locked up after the death of his wife, Caroline, in 1737. Much work was carried out on the palace gardens during his reign, including the creation of the round pond in Kensington Gardens.

After George II died at the palace on 25 October 1760, it fell into disrepair. George III preferred Buckingham Palace and was only interested in Kensington Palace for its art treasures, many of which he began to transfer to other royal palaces. It gradually became denuded and neglected until the end of the 18th century, when accommodation was needed for members of the royal family. Lavish amounts of money were then spent on refurbishment.

The wayward duke

One of the new residents was Edward, Duke of Kent. He was the fourth son of George III and, like his brother, the Prince Regent, had a marked ability to run up massive debts, which resulted in his having to leave the country for Brussels in 1816. Long before this embarrassing event took place, he insisted that his new residence should undergo extensive building work; this was carried out by James Wyatt. Among the rooms that were created was the Red Saloon on the ground floor.

When the Duke of Kent moved into Kensington Palace he was a bachelor, but the sudden death of Princess Charlotte, daughter of the prince regent, in 1817 concentrated his mind on marriage.

In 1818, the Duke of Kent married Victoria, the German Dowager Princess of Leiningen. Their only child, Princess Victoria, was born at Kensington Palace on 24 May 1819, and the family continued to live there. Sadly, the duke died a few months later, in January 1820, shortly before the death of his father.

Victoria

Princess Victoria grew up in Kensington Palace and, when her uncle, William IV, died in the early hours of 20 June 1837, she held her first privy council as queen in the Red Saloon on the same day. She and her mother moved to Buckingham Palace the following month and she wrote in her journal: 'It is not without feelings of regret that I shall bid adieu forever to this my birthplace, to which I am really attached.'

With the sudden departure of Queen Victoria, Kensington Palace once again fell into disrepair. It became a repository for anything valuable that was not wanted in other palaces, and it also developed dry rot. By the 1890s the fate of the palace hung in the balance, with suggestions that it be pulled down, but eventually Parliament paid for its restoration with the proviso that it be opened to the public.

The King's Grand Staircase

Originally built for William III by Sir Christopher Wren in 1689, the King's

▶ *Queen Victoria's bedroom is full of her personal mementoes, including portraits of her children and a bust of Prince Albert.*

Grand Staircase was used by people visiting the king. The simple, plain walls and oak treads were altered in George I's reign into what we see today: the trompe l'oeil on the walls was painted by William Kent and shows an arcaded gallery crammed with George I's courtiers. The ceiling is painted to look like a dome. Anyone visiting the king would first have had to pass the 40 Yeomen of the Guard who thronged the guard chamber on the ground floor, before climbing the King's Grand Staircase and meeting more Yeomen at the top.

The King's Presence Chamber

After walking up the Grand Staircase, visitors then entered the King's Presence Chamber. This room was as imposing and lavish as possible in order to impress upon visitors the might and majesty of the king. In the 18th century the central focus was the throne, which was placed under a decorative damask canopy. The walls were previously hung with tapestries, but are now decorated with 17th-century silk embroideries. The most striking feature is the remarkable ceiling painted by William Kent in 1724 in the 'grotesque' style that was so fashionable at the time. It is square and divided by four red diagonals with a central roundel showing Apollo, the sun god, riding in his chariot. The choice of god was no accident; it implied that George I was the Apollo of his day.

The inner sanctum
In the 18th century, a royal palace was full of people going about their business. Courtiers attended to the needs of the royal family, a string of visitors called on the king and queen, and the royal household made sure that life ran as smoothly as possible. The king and queen had a number of state rooms in which they received their guests, who in turn measured their status by how far they were able to penetrate the inner sanctum of the palace. Some only got as far as the King's Presence Chamber but others who were better dressed were received in the King's Privy Chamber, and courtiers would meet the king in the King's Drawing Room.

KENSINGTON PALACE 93

The Cupola Room

The first room to be decorated by William Kent for George I was the Cupola Room and the work was carried out in 1722. This was the main stateroom, used for the most important occasions, so it was essential that it should look the part. Kent chose the theme of Ancient Rome, with its implication that George was a latter-day Caesar. In order to stress George's legal right to the British throne, Kent painted the Star of the Order of the Garter in the centre of the ceiling. Today, the room is dominated by the clock, made by Charles Clay and John Pyke, which belonged to Augusta, Princess of Wales, the mother of George III.

The Drawing Room

The King's Drawing Room was the most important of the state apartments because

▼ *The cosy, intimate atmosphere of Queen Mary's Dining Room underlines the fact that it was a private room. The Chinese porcelain on the black lacquer cabinet is similar to that collected by Mary II.*

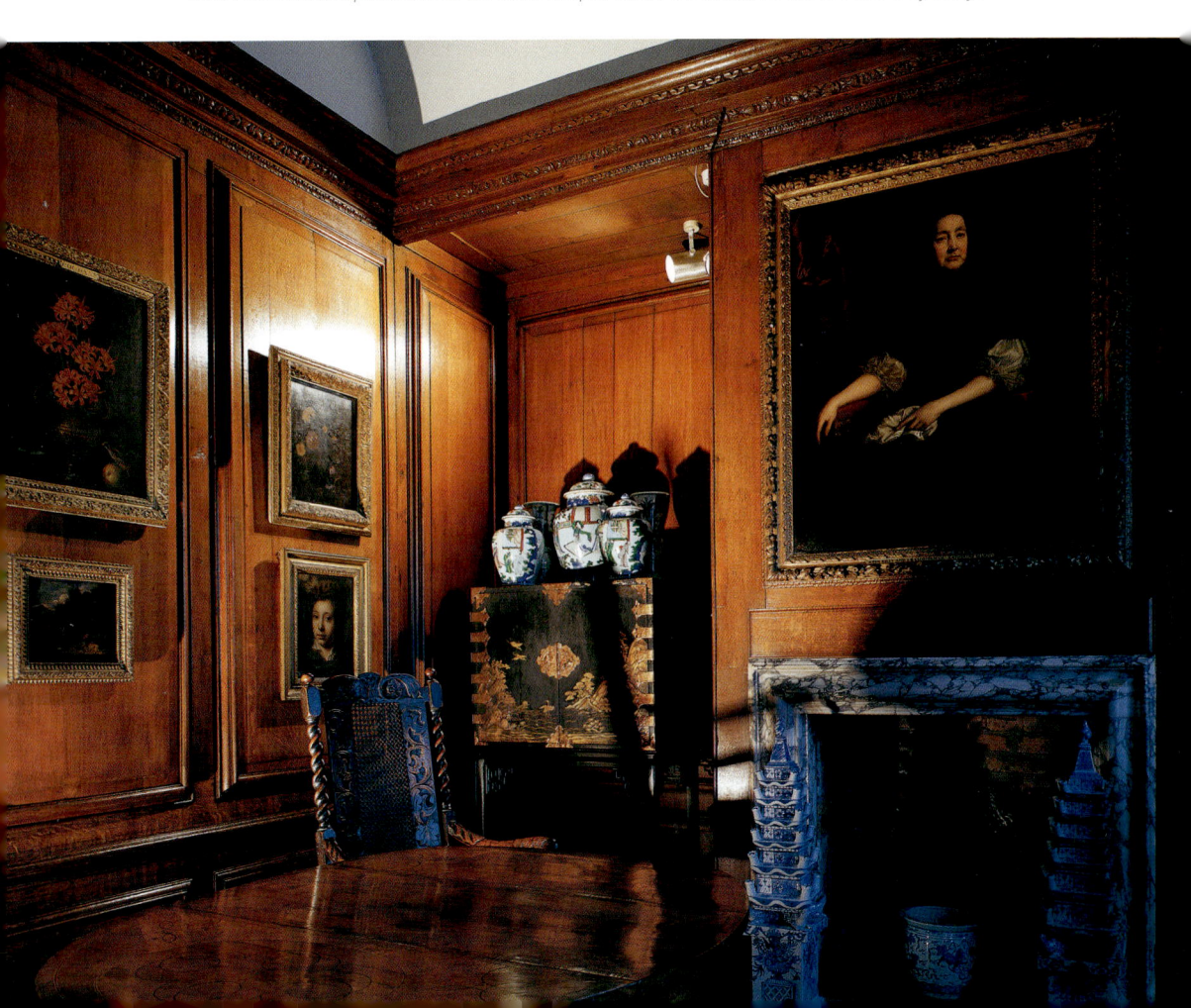

it was the pivot of court life. This was where most of the king's subjects would see him. In fact, it served as an unofficial demarcation line because only courtiers and advisors could penetrate further into the palace. The ceiling, painted by William Kent in 1723, shows Jupiter, which was yet another flattering comparison to George I.

Queen Victoria's Bedroom

The young Princess Victoria was woken in her bedroom on the morning of the death of her uncle, William IV, on 20 June 1837, to be told that she was now queen.

Another queen made her first appearance in this room 30 years later in 1867, when the Duchess of Teck (a granddaughter of George III) gave birth to her daughter, Victoria Mary. She grew up to marry George V, the grandson of Queen Victoria, and became Queen Mary. As Queen Mary she took an active interest in Kensington Palace and was responsible for the redecoration in 1932–3 of Queen Victoria's Bedroom, the ante-room and the Duchess of Kent's Dressing Room.

Queen Mary's Gallery

The Gallery was named after Mary II, wife of William III of Orange. It was an important room for her, as it was where Mary enjoyed her many hobbies. She had been a great collector of porcelain since 1677, when she married William. Items from her extensive collection were arranged in as many places in the palace as possible. They also adorned Mary's other homes at Het Loo and Honselersdijk in the Netherlands, and at Hampton Court, where many pieces are still on show. After Mary's early death in 1694, William shipped her porcelain collection from Kensington Palace to the house of his dear friend, Arnold Joost van Keppel, in The Hague.

Together, the aforementioned rooms create a memorable picture of life in a palace that was partly private home and partly a building in which state business was carried out.

information

Contact details

Kensington Palace State Apartments
Kensington Gardens
London
W8 4PX

0844 482 7777 (from the UK);
+44 (0)20 3166 6000 (from outside the UK)

Historical Royal Palaces site
www.hrp.org.uk/Kensington Palace

Transport links

High Street Kensington (10–15-minute walk); Queensway (10–15-minute walk) or Notting Hill Gate (20–25-minute walk)

70, 94, 148, 390 to Bayswater Road; 9, 10, 49, 52, 70, and 452 to Kensington High Street

ST JAMES'S PALACE
London

KEY DATES

- 1532–40 St James's Palace built for Henry VIII
- 1820–4 John Nash renovates the state apartments
- 1825–7 Clarence House built for the Duke of Clarence by John Nash
- 1841–61 Victoria, Duchess of Kent, lives at Clarence House
- 1866–1900 The Duke and Duchess of Edinburgh live there
- 1900–42 The Duke and Duchess of Connaught live at Clarence House
- 1949–52 Princess Elizabeth and Philip, Duke of Edinburgh, live at Clarence House
- 1950 Princess Anne is born at Clarence House on 15 August
- 1953–2002 The Queen Mother lives at Clarence House
- 2003 The Princes Charles, William and Harry move there
- 2003 Clarence House opened to the public on 6 August

The Court of St James, the official name for the British court, is administered from St James's Palace in London, even though the official residence of the British sovereign is Buckingham Palace. Whenever a new sovereign accedes to the throne, the proclamation is still made from St James's Palace. This somewhat confusing state of affairs dates from the reign of George III. He bought what was then Buckingham House in the 1760s as his private residence, but it was too small to be a fully functioning palace and so the court continued to operate from St James's Palace.

The Tudors

St James's Palace was built between 1532 and 1540 for Henry VIII on the site of a leper hospital for young women called St James's Hospital. The adjoining marshland was drained and turned into St James's Park. The only surviving part of Henry's original palace is the turreted gatehouse to Colour Court, which stands at the southern end of St James's. His daughter, Queen Mary I, had a particular fondness for the palace and it was here, in 1558, that she signed the treaty that gave Calais back to the French, an event which made her so unhappy that she declared 'when I am dead and opened you will find Calais lying in my heart'. Mary died at St James's Palace on 17 November that same year. Her half-sister, Elizabeth I, did not share Mary's

▶ *The Armoury Room has intricately decorated wall panels and a Tudor fireplace, and is adorned with a variety of weapons.*

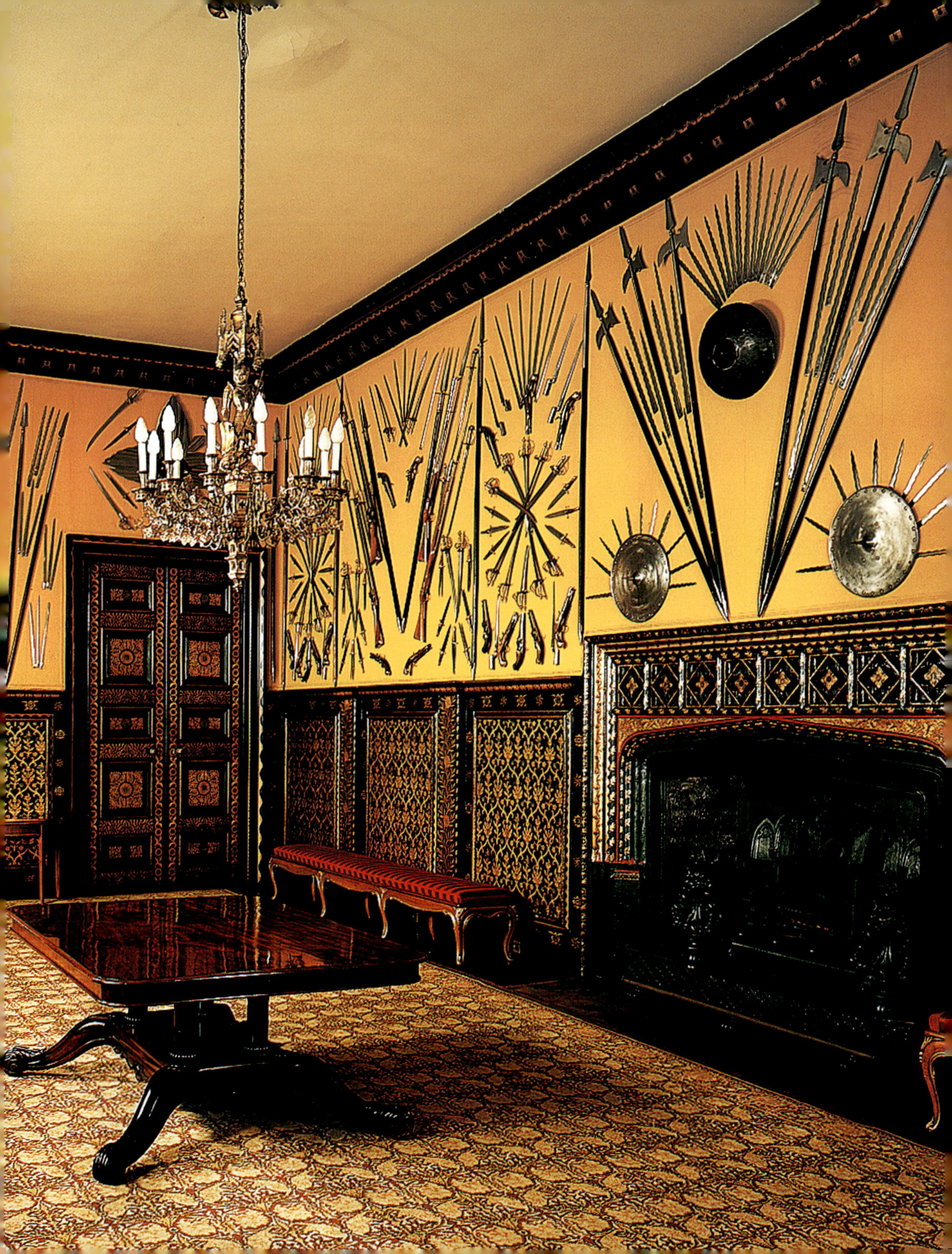

enthusiasm for the palace but she stayed there whenever Whitehall Palace was being cleaned. In July 1588, during the time of the Spanish Armada, Elizabeth moved from Richmond Palace to St James's Palace, which was considered to offer greater security.

Prison, prostitutes and turnips

On occasion, St James's Palace was also used as a place of imprisonment. On 29 January 1649 Charles I spent his last night at the palace, and the following morning was led from it through St James's Park to his execution at the Banqueting House. The previous year, Charles's younger son, the Duke of York (later James II), was also held captive at the palace but escaped during a game of hide-and-seek with his siblings.

In 1698, Whitehall Palace was destroyed by fire and St James's Palace became the main royal residence in London. Queen Anne was born there on 6 February 1665 and spent a great deal of time there during her lifetime. St James's Park had increased in size over the years and was now open to the public, although by Anne's reign it was a notorious haunt for prostitutes. Anne died in 1714 and George I succeeded to the throne. He had a tremendous passion

▼ *The oldest part of St James's Palace is the Tudor gatehouse that leads to Colour Court, which was built for Henry VIII.*

for agriculture and is reputed to have asked a minister how much it would cost to close St James's Park to the public and grow turnips there instead. The ironic answer was: 'Only three crowns, Sire.'

In 1814, during the celebrations following the defeat of Napoleon, the Prussian Colonel-in-Chief, Marshal Blücher, stayed at St James's Palace. The public could see in through the windows of his apartment and it is said he enjoyed bowing to those who strolled past.

> ### INTERESTING FEATURES
> - The Tudor Gatehouse of St James's Palace
> - The Horse Corridor in Clarence House
> - The Garden Room in Clarence House
> - St James's Park

The monarch moves out of the palace

George IV had little interest in the palace, being caught up in more exciting projects, such as the building of Buckingham Palace and the renovations at Windsor Castle. However, he did commission John Nash to remodel the state apartments between 1820 and 1824. George certainly had no intention of living there himself, thereby setting a precedent that was followed by all succeeding monarchs.

Nevertheless, two of George's brothers lived in houses built on opposite sides of Stable Yard Road within the precincts of the palace: the Duke of York lived at York House (which later became Stafford House and is now known as Lancaster House) and the Duke of Clarence (who became William IV in 1830) was installed at Clarence House, which was built specially for him by John Nash between 1825 and 1827. The architecture of Clarence House was markedly different from that of St James's Palace, which had retained its Tudor appearance despite the work of later architects such as John Vanbrugh and Nicholas Hawksmoor. William IV continued to live at Clarence House throughout his seven-year reign, and a first-floor passage was built to link his home with the state apartments in St James's Palace. The king could not abide Buckingham Palace and had attempted to live in St James's Palace, but found it was so small that he and his wife, Queen Adelaide, had to move all their books and letters out of their rooms before they could hold any levées.

The Chapel Royal

Today, St James's Palace is the London residence of the Princess Royal and also of Princess Alexandra. It is a working palace, housing several official departments. The palace also contains the Chapel Royal, which was built by Henry VIII and renovated in 1836. The term 'Chapel Royal' originally did not refer to a chapel itself but to the priests and singers who catered for a king or queen's spiritual needs. The Chapel Royal at St James's Palace has therefore seen some very illustrious musicians in its time, including Henry Purcell, who lived in the palace, and George Handel.

Clarence House

Various members of royalty have made Clarence House their home: Queen Victoria's mother, the Duchess of Kent; Victoria's second son, Alfred, Duke of Edinburgh; and her third son, the Duke of Connaught.

In June 1949 it became the London home of the then Princess Elizabeth and

◄ *Official functions and formal addresses to visiting foreign heads of government are conducted in the Throne Room at St James's Palace.*

Prince Philip, Duke of Edinburgh. Before they moved in it needed complete renovation, which was complicated by post-war rationing and bomb damage. All the Victorian decorations were removed and replaced with a modern, clean, unfussy look. Princess Elizabeth became Elizabeth II on 6 February 1952, following the death of her father, George VI. She moved with her young family to Buckingham Palace. Clarence House was prepared for Elizabeth II's mother, now the Queen Mother, who moved there with her younger daughter, Princess Margaret, in May 1953. Clarence House remained the London home of the Queen Mother until her death on 30 March 2002. It then became the London home of Prince Charles and his sons, the Princes William and Harry. It was extensively renovated and in summer 2003, Prince Charles opened some of the rooms to the public for the first time.

information

Contact details

St James's Palace
Westminster
London SW1A 1AA

+44 (0)20 7930 1793

Official site of the Royal Monarchy
www.royal.gov.uk/TheRoyal
Residences/StJamessPalace
/StJamessPalace.aspx

Transport links

Green Park

THE PALACE OF WESTMINSTER
London

KEY DATES

✠ **1040–66** First palace built by Edward the Confessor

✠ **1097** Present palace begun by William Rufus

✠ **Until 1882** The Law Courts were situated in Westminster Hall for 600 years

✠ **1547** Royal Chapel of St Stephen secularized

✠ **1550 onwards** House of Commons meets in the palace

✠ **1834** The Houses of Parliament almost totally destroyed by fire

✠ **1837–60** The new Houses of Parliament built by Charles Barry and Augustus Pugin

✠ **1941** House of Commons destroyed in an air raid on 10 May

The Palace of Westminster has a long and varied history. It was originally the main residence of English monarchs, a purpose it fulfilled for nearly 400 years before catching fire in 1512 and forcing Henry VIII to decamp to Whitehall Palace. The medieval palace was almost completely destroyed in another fire in 1834 and the buildings erected in its place are still known collectively as the Palace of Westminster. They are the seat of the British Parliament, housing both the House of Commons and the House of Lords, as well as offices for all members of Parliament.

Edward the Confessor
The first palace to stand on this site on the banks of the River Thames was a large rectangular fortified building with a moat, built in the 11th century for Edward the Confessor. At the time, this area was known as Thorney, which meant 'island of briars'. The palace was built on marshland and its proximity to the River Thames gave it strategic importance at a period when water was a very efficient means of transportation. Another favourable aspect was that it was far enough away from the rest of London for the reigning monarch to feel safe whenever trouble brewed with his subjects. Edward's palace was also close to the monastery he had built, which today we know as Westminster Abbey. Edward the Confessor died in the palace at the beginning of 1066 and in doing so set off a sudden chain of revolutionary events in the

▶ *Today the site of the Houses of Parliament, the Palace of Westminster is one of the most magnificent sights in London.*

THE PALACE OF WESTMINSTER

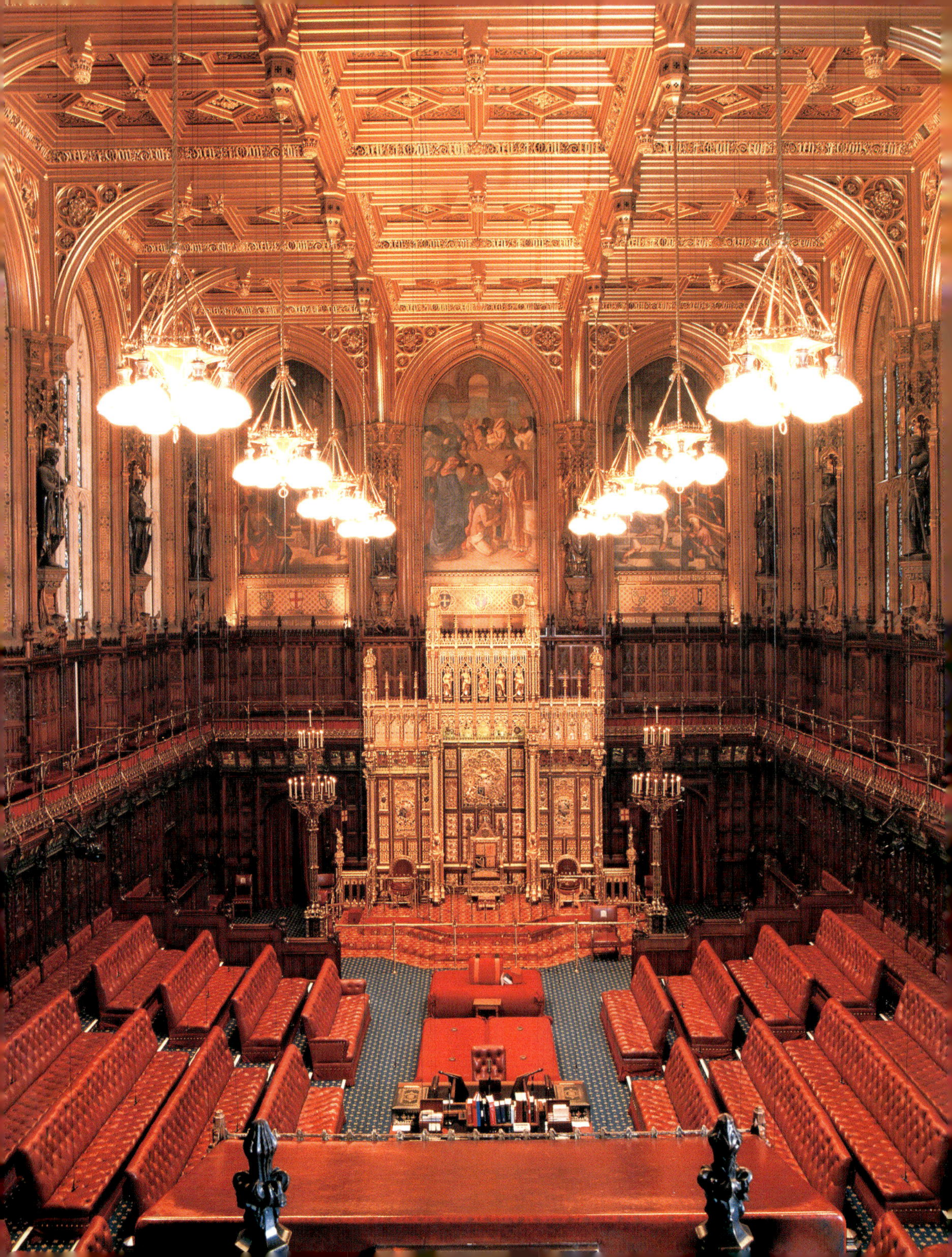

The Lord's Chamber in the House of Lords is also known as the Upper House. The Queen attends the State Opening of Parliament here.

country: by the end of that year, England had had three successive kings and had also been invaded by the Normans.

William the Conqueror

Before he died, Edward had named his brother-in-law, Harold, Earl of Wessex, as his successor. Harold was crowned King of England in January 1066, but there were others who also believed they had been promised the English throne, most notably William, Duke of Normandy. William was fully prepared to fight for what he wanted, so he raised an army, sailed to the south coast of England and defeated Harold at the Battle of Hastings in October of that year. In one fell swoop, William ended the dynasty of Saxon kings that had ruled England for so long. He united England with Normandy and introduced many French customs and ideas. Above all, he knew he had to subjugate his new kingdom in order to control it, and this he did with a heavy hand. First, however, William had to make his new position official, so he had himself crowned in Westminster Abbey on Christmas Day, 1066, just over two months after his victory at the Battle of Hastings. His coronation set a precedent, as it was the first to be carried out in Westminster Abbey; since then, virtually every British monarch has been crowned there.

Westminster Hall

William moved into Westminster Palace and, in due course, his son William Rufus took up residence there as William II. He wanted to enlarge and improve the palace, but he only had time to build Westminster

---

INTERESTING FEATURES

- *Hammerbeam roof in Westminster Hall*
- *Frescoes depicting Arthurian legends in Robing Room*
- *Perpendicular Gothic architecture of the Houses of Parliament*
- *Big Ben in St Stephen's Tower*
- *The buildings in Old Palace Yard*
- *The Jewel Tower, one of the last remaining buildings of the original Palace of Westminster*
- *The Strangers' Galleries, where the public can sit in the House of Commons*

Hall before his untimely death in 1100. This was a period of English history when kings and heirs seemed happy to plot against their rivals, and William is believed to have been shot in the back by a supporter of his younger brother, Henry, who promptly inherited the crown and became Henry I.

Westminster Hall was built at the northern end of the palace, with the domestic apartments situated at the eastern and southern ends, and is the only part of the original palace that is still standing. When Westminster Hall was completed in 1099, William Rufus complained about its size, saying that it was a 'mere bedchamber' in comparison to what he had been expecting. This was some bedchamber: the Hall consisted of a central nave 73 metres (240 ft) long, almost 12 metres (40 ft) high and with a gallery that ran all around it. The walls were over 1.8 metres (6 ft) thick. At the time, it was the largest hall in Europe. Succeeding kings have also made their mark on it: Edward II had it restored after a fire in 1291 and Richard II increased the height of the palace walls by 0.6 metres (2 ft). He was also responsible for construction of the oak hammerbeam roof, which is 28 metres (92 ft) high in the centre and was a magnificent feat of medieval architecture. It is still one of the largest unsupported roofs in the world.

Although Westminster Hall was originally used as a banqueting hall,

▶ *The Arthurian frescoes in the Queen's Robing Room were painted by William Dyce in 1841 after he successfully competed for the honour.*

particularly for coronations, between the 13th and 19th centuries it also contained the Law Courts. Curiously, these were joined in the mid 1600s by stalls selling a variety of goods, including books. On occasion, the traders would conduct their business as usual while momentous events in English history were taking place in the nearby courts. The trials of Sir Thomas More and Anne Boleyn, who both fell foul of Henry VIII, were held there in 1535 and 1536 respectively, and Guy Fawkes also stood trial there in 1606 after his abortive attempt to blow up the House of Commons with the king and Parliament inside. In 1649, in a trial that would forever change the relationship between the English people and their monarch, Charles I was convicted of treason in the Palace of Westminster and sentenced to death.

Westminster Hall is still in use today as the vestibule of the House of Commons. It featured prominently in 1979 during celebrations to mark the Queen's Silver Jubilee, and again in 1995 during the 50th anniversary celebrations to mark the end of the Second World War. It has also been the location of the lying-in-state of several prominent figures: Edward VII in 1910, Sir Winston Churchill in 1965, and Queen Elizabeth the Queen Mother in 2002.

The Vision of Sir Galahad **RELIGION** and his Company

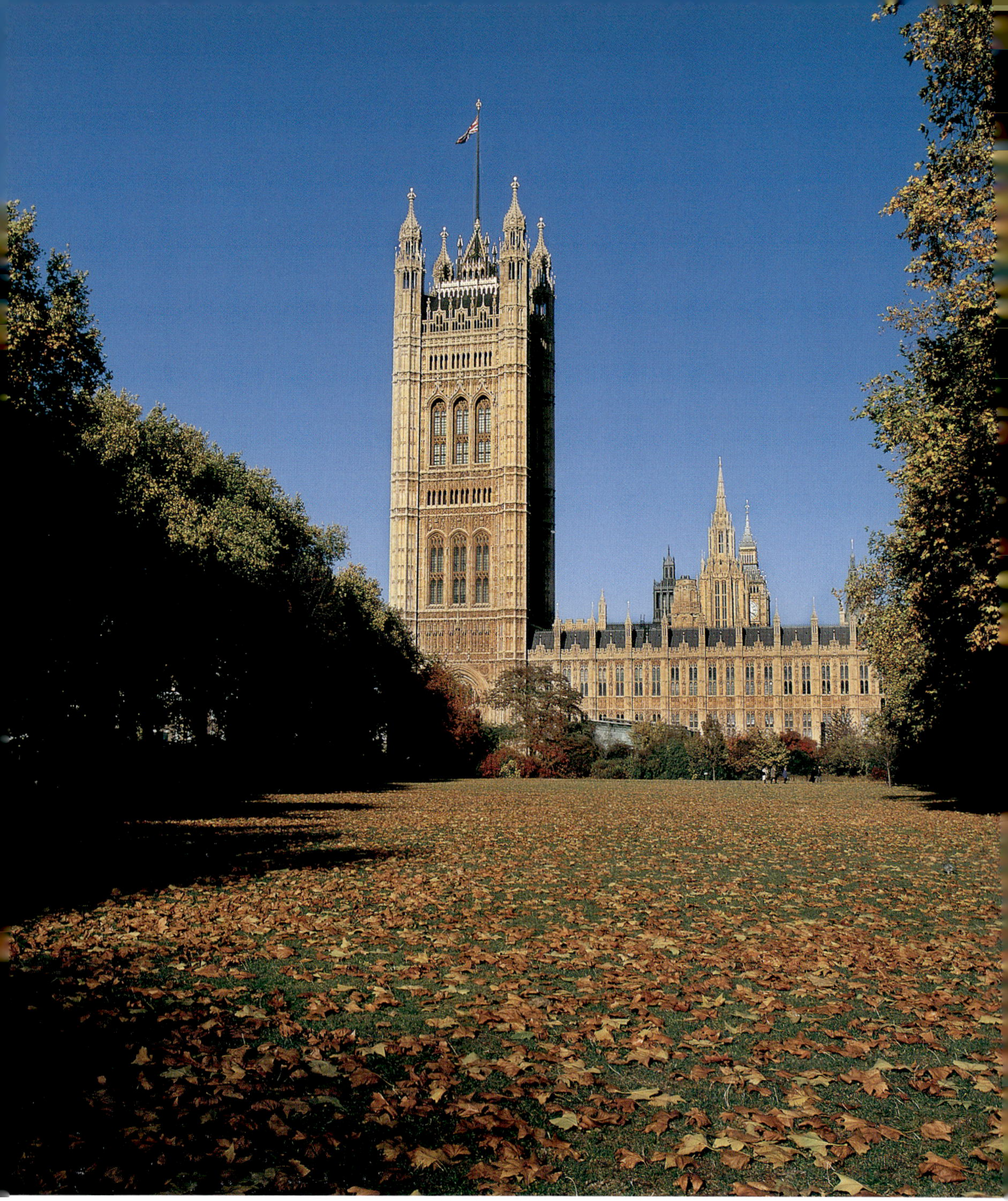

The Victoria Tower Gardens take their name from the Victoria Tower, which overlooks the gardens from the Palace of Westminster.

The British parliamentary system

The palace has seen the development of the British parliamentary system, which is widely copied throughout the world. During medieval times the palace was not only the home of the reigning sovereign, it was also the site of Parliament and the Law Courts, and the buildings were designed accordingly. The monarch was advised by the Royal Council, which consisted of bishops and nobles. This eventually led to the formation of the House of Lords. The House of Commons was the natural development of a council of lesser personages, such as burgesses and knights, who began to meet independently of the Royal Council. From 1550, the House of Commons met in what had been the Royal Chapel of St Stephen until it was deconsecrated in 1547.

One of the few areas of the Palace of Westminster that has survived over the centuries is Old Palace Yard. It has been the address of some notable people, including the writers Geoffrey Chaucer, when he was Clerk of the King's Works, and Ben Jonson. Old Palace Yard has also been the site of executions such as those of Guy Fawkes and Sir Walter Raleigh.

Fire at the palace

Various fires have destroyed much of the original medieval palace. In 1512, following a fire, Henry VIII moved out of the Palace of Westminster into Whitehall Palace. He was the last sovereign to live at the palace and the royal apartments were taken over by parliamentary officials. Nevertheless, the building continued to be called a royal palace and is still regarded as such today.

In October 1834 fire once again swept through the medieval palace, and this time it was virtually destroyed; only the crypt of St Stephen's Chapel, the Jewel Tower and Westminster Hall survived. This was disastrous, but it was also an opportunity for some imaginative redevelopment. Charles Barry and Augustus Pugin were the architects, and they created the Gothic buildings that we know today.

information

Contact details

The Palace of Westminster
20 Dean's Yard
City of London SW1P 3PA

+44 (0)20 7219 3000

UK Parliament site
www.parliament.uk/about/living-heritage/building/palace

Transport links

Victoria, Charing Cross, Waterloo

Westminster, Victoria, Charing Cross, Waterloo

THE PALACE OF WESTMINSTER

ELTHAM PALACE
Eltham

KEY DATES

✠ *1305 The moated manor house is given to Edward II*

✠ *1402 Henry IV married to Joan of Navarre by proxy at the palace on 3 April*

✠ *1470s The Great Hall built*

✠ *1650s Eltham Palace seized by Parliament*

✠ *1827 Preservation campaign mounted to save the Great Barn*

✠ *1936 Modern Art Deco house completed*

✠ *1944–92 Army educational units occupy Eltham*

✠ *1995 English Heritage take over the property*

✠ *1999 Major restoration of the property completed*

✠ *2000 New garden designed by Isabelle Van Groeningen opens*

There have been two great flowerings in the life of Eltham Palace. The first lasted for three centuries between the reigns of Edward II and Elizabeth I, when it was considered one of the great medieval English palaces. The second occurred in the 1930s, when the Courtauld family, the people who lived there at the time, turned it into a fine example of Art Deco splendour. Today, Eltham Palace offers an extraordinary contrast of styles, each richly evocative of particular periods in English history.

Medieval royalty

Eltham, located in what is now a busy suburb of Greater London, has the distinction of being mentioned in the Domesday Book as the property of Odo, Bishop of Bayeux (the half-brother of William the Conqueror). At this time a moated manor house stood on the site, which was given to Edward II when he was still Prince of Wales in 1305. In due course the house passed to his French wife, Queen Isabella, who spent much of her time at Eltham Palace. Known in her own lifetime as the 'She Wolf of France', Isabella was an ambitious and scheming woman. Edward's marriage to her ensured an alliance with the French, as her father was King Philip IV of France, but it also eventually resulted in Edward's murder at Berkeley Castle, over which Isabella conspired with her lover, Roger Mortimer, an exiled opponent of Edward.

▸ *The Great Hall, with its hammerbeam roof and oriel windows, has miraculously survived an eventful history.*

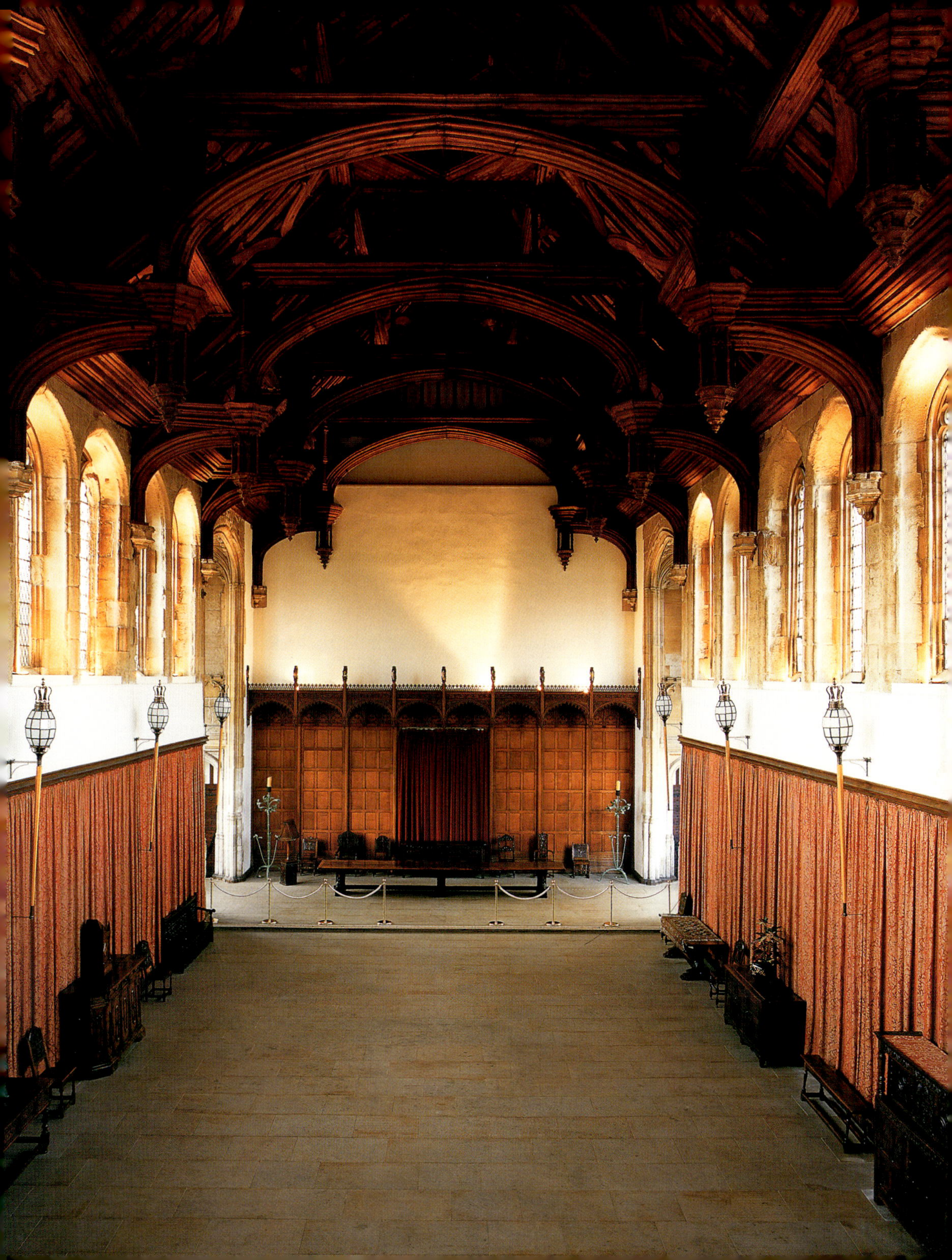

During the reign of Richard II, in the 14th century, improvements were made to Eltham Palace under the guidance of Geoffrey Chaucer, who was the Clerk of Works. After Richard's death (in 1400), Henry IV was married by proxy at Eltham Palace to Joan of Navarre in 1402.

Some of the most significant changes to Eltham Palace were carried out by Edward IV during his reign, including the building of the Great Hall in the 1470s. This room has the third largest hammerbeam roof in the country, and was the scene of many royal celebrations and feasts.

Henry VIII spent a large part of his boyhood at Eltham Palace. He was the last monarch to invest financially in the palace, but as he got older he spent less time at Eltham. His daughter, Elizabeth I, became an infrequent visitor, as she preferred to be at Greenwich Palace, which was situated nearby. While Greenwich Palace retained its importance during Elizabeth I's long reign, the palace at Eltham was neglected.

> The Courtaulds' modernist 1930s house, designed by Seely and Paget, adjoins the medieval Great Hall.

Leaving royal hands

Eltham Palace passed out of royal hands altogether during the interregnum that followed the execution of Charles I in 1649, as it was seized by Parliament. By this time it was described as being 'much out of repair', and was sold to Colonel Nathaniel Rich, who began to demolish it. After visiting the palace in 1656, the diarist John Evelyn recorded: 'Both the palace and chapel in miserable ruins, the noble wood and park destroyed by Rich, the Rebel.' In the early 19th century, the then owner, Sir John Shaw, left the remains of the palace to moulder and built Eltham Lodge in the grounds instead. He used the Great Hall as a barn, a function that it continued to perform for the next two centuries, even after a campaign to protect it from demolition in 1827.

A renaissance at Eltham

The renaissance of Eltham Palace began in the 1930s when a wealthy couple, Stephen and Virginia Courtauld, bought it and built a highly contemporary house next to the Great Hall. The house was the last word in Art Deco architecture and formed a stunning contrast to the splendours of the medieval hall that stood beside it. The Courtaulds paid equal attention to the gardens and laid out a

---

INTERESTING FEATURES

✠ The Great Hall
✠ The 1930s tearoom
✠ The gardens

sunken rose garden, a rock garden, a spring bulb meadow and a woodland garden. They left Eltham Palace in 1944, when it was taken over by army educational units that stayed until 1992.

In 1995 English Heritage acquired Eltham Palace and spent four years restoring it before opening it to the public, in all its medieval and Art Deco beauty, in 1999.

information

Contact details

Eltham Palace
Eltham, Greenwich
London SE9 5QE

+44 (0)208 294 2548

English Heritage
www.english-heritage.org.uk
/daysout/properties/eltham-palace-and-gardens

Transport links

Eltham and Mottingham, both 0.8 km (½ mile)

126, 161

Access off Court Road SE9, junction 3 on the M25, then the A20 to Eltham

THE BANQUETING HOUSE
London

KEY DATES

✠ **14th century** The Archbishops of York build York Place

✠ **1514** Cardinal Thomas Wolsey moves into York Place

✠ **1529** Wolsey gives York Place to Henry VIII on 22 October

✠ **1619** Banqueting House destroyed by fire on 12 January

✠ **1622** Replacement Banqueting House, designed by Inigo Jones, is finished

✠ **1636** Installation of nine ceiling panels, painted by Rubens, in March

✠ **1649** Execution of Charles I on 30 January

✠ **1893–1962** The Royal United Services Institute uses the Banqueting House as a museum

✠ Restoration for the 400th anniversary

The Banqueting House in Whitehall, London, is an exquisite gem of royal architecture. Inigo Jones built it between 1619 and 1622, and it was at the forefront of an architectural revolution that gradually transformed London from a medieval jumble of timber and brick houses to a city of stone buildings inspired by Ancient Rome and contemporary Italian design. Charles I's execution there in 1649 threw Britain into a decade of republicanism and was a turning point in the relationship between the British monarchy and its parliament: from the Restoration in 1660 onwards, the balance of power changed forever.

From palace to Banqueting House

The Banqueting House is all that remains of the medieval Whitehall Palace built by Henry VIII. He acquired what was then York Place, the official London residence of the Archbishops of York, as a penance from Cardinal Thomas Wolsey in 1529. Henry moved into York Place within 10 days, renamed it Whitehall and began a massive expansion programme. By the time Henry died in 1547, Whitehall was the biggest palace in Europe, stretching for 9 hectares (22 acres).

In 1581, a timber and canvas banqueting house was built for Elizabeth I on the site of the present building and this was still standing, in a much-dilapidated state,

▶ *Inigo Jones gave the Banqueting Hall Room classical proportions, making it twice as long as it is wide and high.*

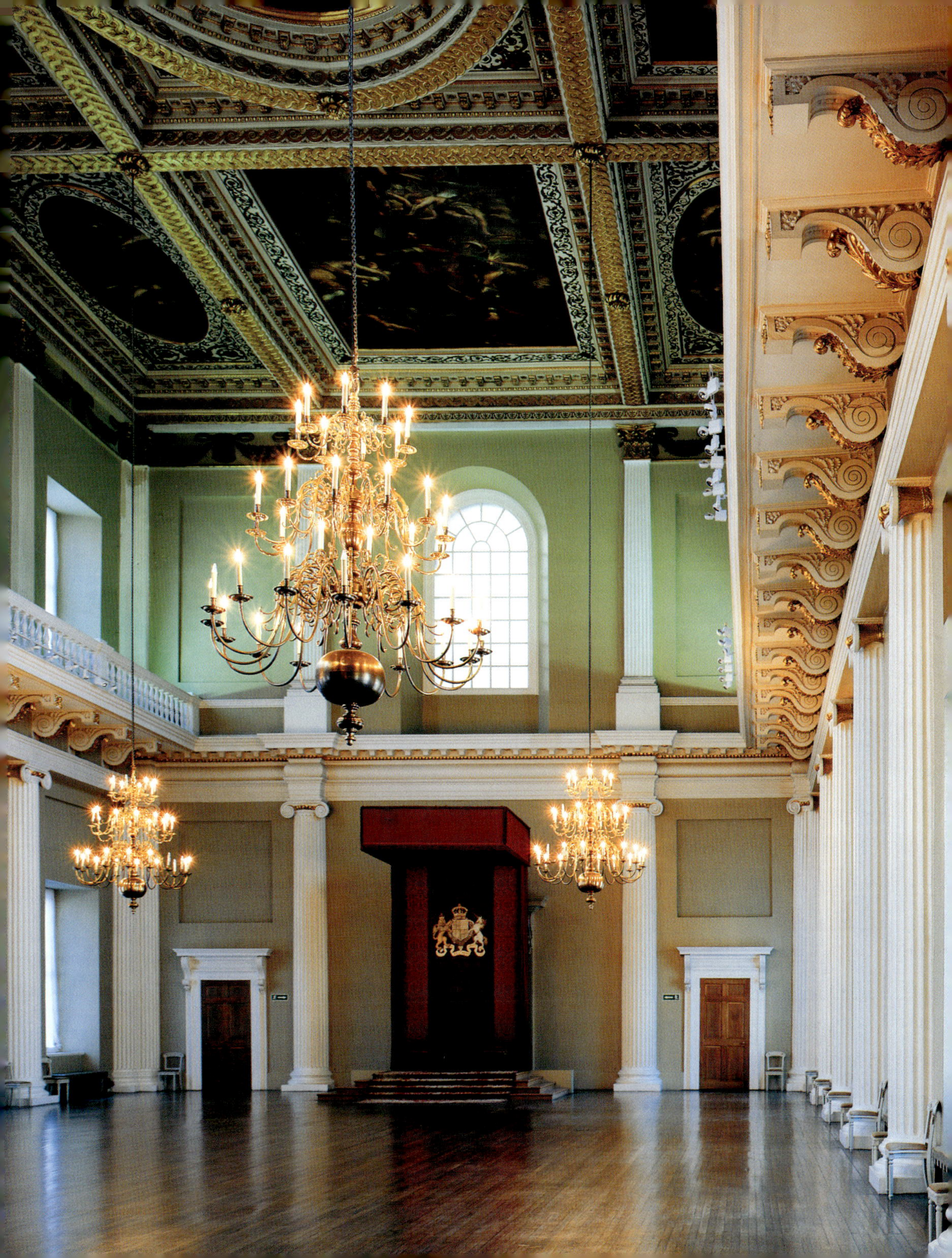

when James I of England and VI of Scotland took the throne in 1603. Three years later, he replaced the old Elizabethan banqueting house with a building specifically for court masques (theatrical and musical entertainment), but this burned down in 1619. James then commissioned Inigo Jones to build a replacement in 1622. Its clean, elegant interior was intended to resemble a Roman basilica, a design on which many Christian churches are based. James's son, Charles I, who commissioned Sir Peter Paul Rubens to paint nine ceiling panels celebrating the life and reign of James I, embellished this. The paintings underlined the Stuart belief in the divine right of kings, the notion that led to Charles's execution.

Execution and restoration
Ironically, no more masques were held in the Banqueting House after the installation of the paintings in 1636, for fear they would be damaged by lamp smoke. A new masque

▶ *The exterior of the Banqueting House was refaced in Portland stone between 1829 and 1837.*

house was built at the back of the Banqueting House, which was used principally for diplomatic functions, when the galleries and floor would be crammed with onlookers. The street outside was also crammed with onlookers on the afternoon of 30 January 1649, when Charles I stepped through a window of the Banqueting House onto a specially built balcony, where he was executed. As the public executioner refused to attend and his assistant could not be found, Charles I was beheaded by two hooded men whose identities were never revealed. It was a bitter winter's day, so Charles wore two shirts in case any shivers should be interpreted as those of fear. When his son, Charles II, was formally restored to the throne on 29 May 1660, his 30th birthday, he was received by both Houses of Parliament at the Banqueting House.

INTERESTING FEATURES

✠ *The commemorative plaque above the entrance*

✠ *The undercroft*

✠ *The nine painted ceiling panels*

✠ *The replica of James I's throne and Canopy of State*

✠ *The Canopy of State in the position occupied by the altar in a church*

The crown was once again offered here on 13 February 1689, when the Prince and Princess of Orange were invited to become William III and Mary II. Whitehall Palace burned down in 1698 and the Banqueting House was converted into a chapel royal. It was used as a museum between 1893 and 1962, but has now been restored to its original glory. It is a small building that has played a major role in British history.

information

Contact details

The Banqueting House
Whitehall
London SW1A 2ER

0844 482 7777 (from UK)
+44 (0)20 3166 6000 (from outside the UK)

Historic Palaces site
www.hrp.org.uk/banquetinghouse

Transport links

Charing Cross

3, 11, 12, 24, 53, 77A, 88 and 159

Westminster, Embankment, Charing Cross

THE BANQUETING HOUSE

THE QUEEN'S HOUSE
Greenwich

Viewed from the River Thames, the beautiful Queen's House in Greenwich is dwarfed by two large flanking wings of what is now the National Maritime Museum – a perfect Palladian house perched between two much bigger buildings.

Medieval palaces

There has been a royal palace at Greenwich since Tudor times; Humphrey, Duke of Gloucester, the brother of Henry V, built the original palace, called Bella Court in 1427. In 1433, it was enhanced by his acquisition of 80 hectares (200 acres) – now Greenwich Park. Henry VIII and his daughters, Mary and Elizabeth, were all born there, in what became one of Henry's favourite palaces.

Inigo Jones and the Civil War

In 1614, James I settled both the park and the palace on his wife, Anne of Denmark, and commissioned Inigo Jones to design a new palace for her. Jones's design was influenced by the architecture of Andrea Palladio in Italy and he began building in 1616. Work stopped two years later when Anne became ill; she died in 1619, and the incomplete building was given to her son, Prince Charles. He became Charles I in 1625 and, four years later, gave the Greenwich palace to his wife, Henrietta Maria, who instructed Jones to continue his work. The house was completed in 1640. She was so charmed by it that she called it 'the house of delight'.

KEY DATES

- 1427 Humphrey, Duke of Gloucester, builds Bella Court
- 1447 Henry VI and Margaret of Anjou acquire it and rename it Placentia
- 1614 James I settles the Manor of Greenwich on Anne of Denmark
- 1616 Inigo Jones begins work on the Queen's House
- 1629 Charles I gives Greenwich to his wife, Henrietta Maria
- 1640 The Queen's House is completed
- 1642 Confiscated by Parliamentary forces
- 1660 Returned to royal ownership at the Restoration
- 1808 Sold to the Royal Naval Asylum
- 1934 Taken over by the National Maritime Museum
- 1984 The Queen's House closed to be reopened in 1990

Leading European painters, including Rubens and Gentileschi of Pisa, were invited to decorate the interior of the Queen's House, but it was barely finished when the Civil War began. Parliamentary forces confiscated it in 1642.

In 1808, it was sold to the Royal Naval Asylum, a school for the orphans of sailors. A year later the colonnades and wings on either side of the house were added. It was taken over by the National Maritime Museum in 1934, and part of it has been restored to its 17th-century splendour.

▲ *Inigo Jones described the Queen's House as 'solid ... masculine and unaffected'.*

INTERESTING FEATURES

✠ *The King's Presence Chamber*

✠ *Modern copies of the Gentileschi panels in the galleried Hall*

✠ *The Tulip Staircase, the earliest cantilevered spiral staircase in Britain (see photograph, page 118)*

information

Contact details

The Queen's House
Park Row
London SE10 9NF

+44 (0)20 8858 4422

National Maritime Museum site
www.nmm.ac.uk/about/history/queens-house

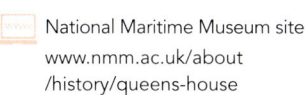

Transport links

Greenwich

North Greenwich

THE QUEEN'S HOUSE

South-west England and Wales

There has been a protracted history of insurrection and warfare along the border between England and Wales. Medieval English kings were anxious to quell costly Welsh uprisings and did so using a variety of measures, but Edward I made an unequivocal statement when he created his 'iron ring' of castles in north Wales at the end of the 13th century. Castles such as Harlech, built by unwelcome English invaders, were bitterly resented by the Welsh people whom they were intended to subdue. Today, these magnificent castles are lasting reminders not only of the tensions between England and Wales but also of the skill of those medieval craftsmen.

▶ *Rising above the land around it, Harlech Castle, in north Wales, has a panoramic view of the surrounding countryside. It was built as one of Edward I's 'iron ring' of castles, which the king believed were essential in conquering north and west Wales.*

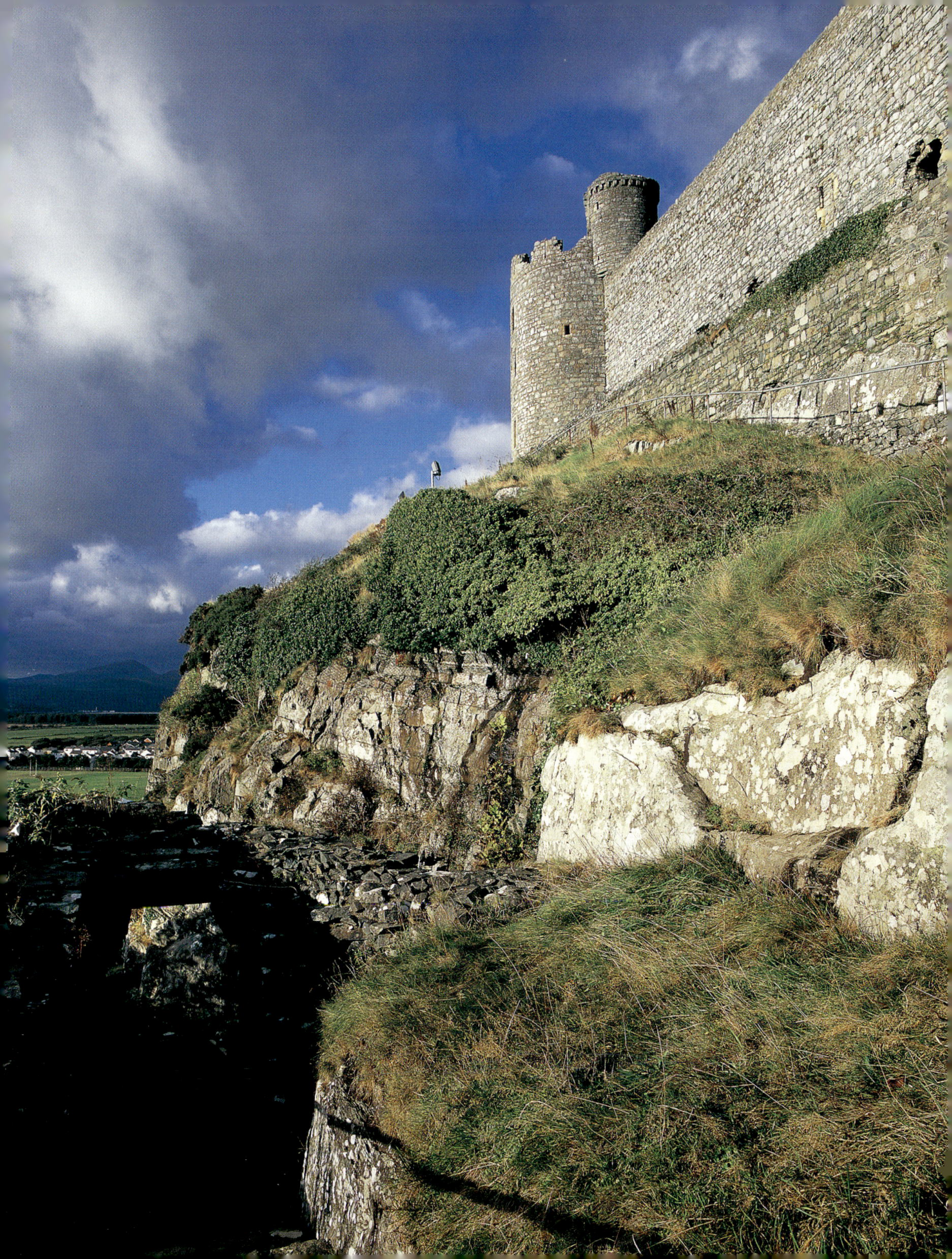

BLENHEIM PALACE
Oxfordshire

Although it is called a palace, Blenheim was not built for a sovereign. It was, however, a royal gift, as Queen Anne awarded £240,000 of her own money to John Churchill, the 1st Duke of Marlborough, towards the building costs. Anne had good reason to be grateful to him, as he had led his troops to a resounding victory over the French forces of Louis XIV at the Battle of Blenheim on the north bank of the Danube in Germany on 13 August 1704.

Blenheim Palace was designed by Sir John Vanbrugh, fresh from completing his previous architectural masterpiece at Castle Howard in Yorkshire. Blenheim was the grandest possible monument to Marlborough's skill as a soldier and the exterior of the palace was adorned with many architectural reminders of the British triumph over the French. In fact, the building was covered with decorations that symbolized Britain's supremacy over her long-standing foe and the interior was equally imposing – more of a national monument to a great hero than an intimate home.

Work on Blenheim began in 1705, but it was beset by problems, many of which stemmed from the close relationship Queen Anne had with the Duke's wife, Sarah. Anne and Sarah had known each other since childhood, and Sarah became a lady of the bedchamber when Anne married Prince George of Denmark in 1683. Anne was concerned about the difference in status between them and suggested that they overcame

▶ *The Great Hall displays Queen Anne's arms on the keystone above the main arch, which encloses a minstrels' gallery.*

KEY DATES

✠ *1650* John Churchill born on 26 May

✠ *1702* John Churchill created 1st Duke of Marlborough

✠ *1704* Battle of Blenheim won by the British on 13 August

✠ *1705* Work starts on Blenheim Palace

✠ *1711* Marlborough dismissed from all his appointments on 31 December

✠ *1712–14* Work on Blenheim suspended

✠ *1716* Sir John Vanbrugh resigns

✠ *1722* Death of Marlborough on 16 June

✠ *1744* Death of Sarah, 1st Duchess of Marlborough, on 18 October

✠ *1764* Capability Brown creates the lake

✠ *1874* Birth of Winston Spencer Churchill at Blenheim on 30 November

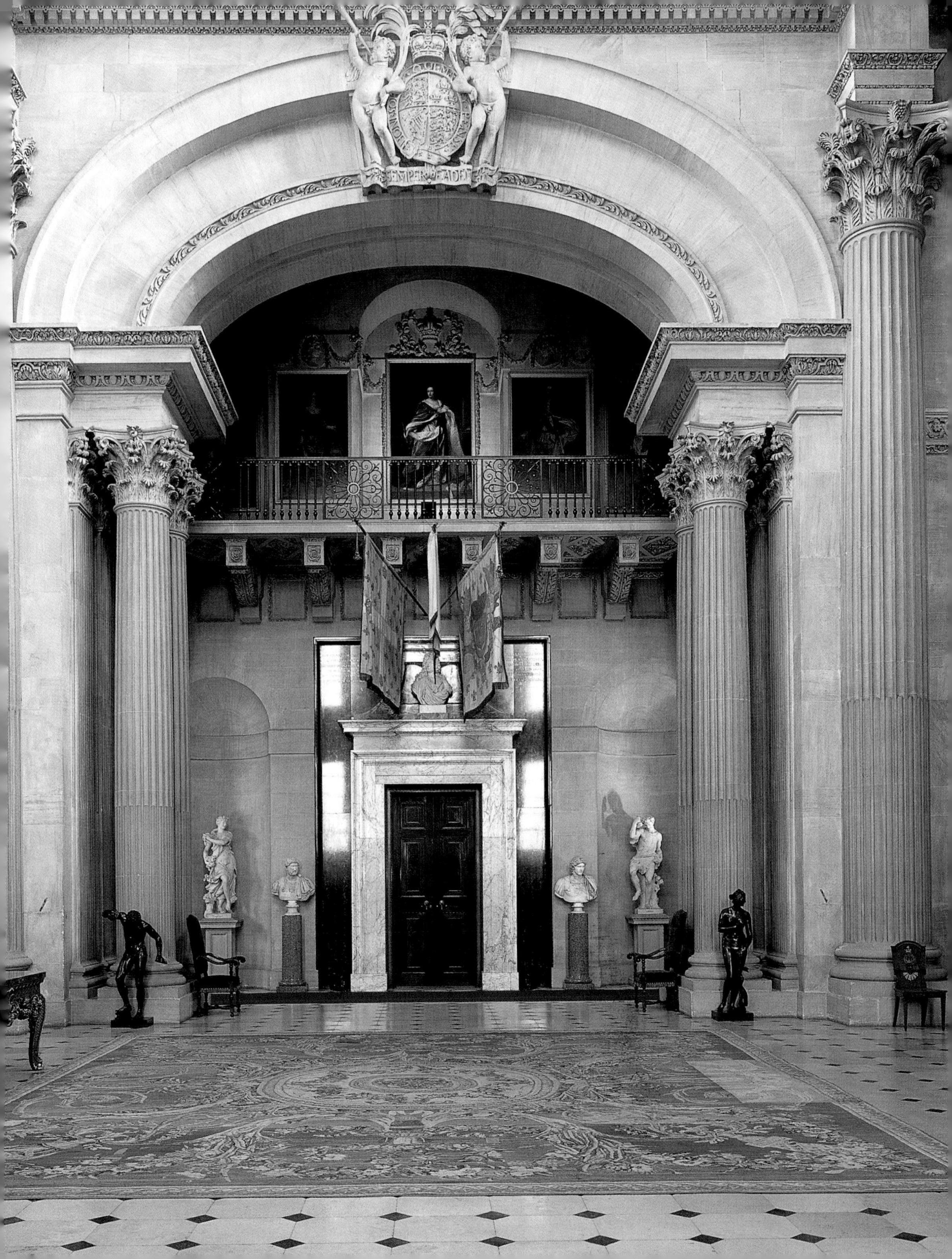

this by calling one another 'Mrs Morley' and 'Mrs Freeman'. Sarah, who assumed the name 'Mrs Freeman' because of what she called her 'frank, open temper', apparently had the upper hand in the relationship as she treated 'Mrs Morley' in a bossy and dictatorial manner. Their relationship came to a sticky end in 1711 when Anne's loyalty switched from Sarah to her cousin, Abigail Masham.

Financial crisis
Falling out of favour with the queen came at a bad time for the Churchills. Marlborough's opponents had been steadily undermining his reputation as a Tory politician while he fought abroad, and in December 1711 he was dismissed from his positions and falsely accused of the misuse of public funds. To add insult to injury, some of the money he had been promised for Blenheim failed to appear. Lacking the £45,000 he needed to pay the builders and craftsmen, work on the palace stopped in 1712. After negotiating with the unpaid workmen two years later, the Duke and Duchess resumed work on the palace with their own money.

The palace was still not finished when the Duke died in 1722. This was deeply provoking to Sarah, who resented having to pay for a house that she considered to be overblown and fussy. In 1716 she had had a massive row with the architect, Vanbrugh, who promptly resigned. The palace was finally completed partly by Nicholas Hawksmoor and partly by James Moore, who had made the mirrors for Blenheim.

Winston Churchill
Sir Winston Churchill, the British Prime Minister, was born at Blenheim on 30 November 1874. He was heir presumptive to Blenheim in the 1890s, but the title then passed to his cousin, the 9th Duke of Marlborough, and it never became his home. In a newspaper

---

INTERESTING FEATURES

- ✠ *The bust of Marlborough, framed by the royal arms, in the Entrance Hall*
- ✠ *The painted walls and ceiling of the Saloon*
- ✠ *The Willis organ in the Long Library*
- ✠ *The bedroom in which Winston Churchill was born*
- ✠ *The water gardens*
- ✠ *The lake*

▲ *The Green Drawing Room still has its original 18th-century ceilings, which were designed by Nicholas Hawksmoor.*

article written in 1966, after Churchill's death, the 10th Duke of Marlborough said, 'Much as Winston cared for Blenheim, it would not have appealed to him to go down in history as its owner – he had other and better ideas.'

ⓘ information

Contact details

Blenheim Palace
Woodstock
Oxfordshire OX20 1PX

+44 (0)1993 810 500
(Freephone 0800 849 6500)

Blenheim Palace
www.blenheimpalace.com

Transport links

🚆 Bicester; Birmingham

🚌 Coach: Gloucester Green (Oxford)

🚍 S3 to Woodstock from Oxford train station and Gloucester Green to gates

🚗 Near Woodstock; 13 km (8 miles) north-west of Oxford on the A44 Evesham Road

BLENHEIM PALACE

BERKELEY CASTLE
Gloucestershire

KEY DATES

✠ 1153 Henry II grants a charter to build a shell-keep

✠ 1215 Barons meet in the Great Hall before signing the Magna Carta

✠ 1327 Murder of Edward II in the King's Gallery on 21 September

✠ 1637 Grand Stairs built

✠ 1641 Sir William Berkeley becomes Governor of Virginia

✠ 1640s The wall of the keep is damaged during the Civil War

✠ Late 1900s Beer is brewed in what is now the outside tearoom and piped to the cellar

Almost 900 years of history have soaked into the walls at Berkeley Castle. It is perhaps not as well known as some other castles, yet so much has happened to it over the centuries that it deserves to be celebrated and recognized as one of the true treasures of Britain. Berkeley was built in the 12th century on the orders of Henry II, who needed a strategically placed castle that not only guarded the Severn Valley but also acted as a defence against the Welsh. In 1153 he granted a charter to Robert Fitzharding to build the shell-keep and the rest of the castle was gradually built around it.

A place in history

Berkeley Castle is the oldest inhabited castle in England and has been the seat of the Berkeley family since it was built. In the 1380s, the chaplain, John Trevisa, believing that the Bible should be translated from Latin into everyday language for everyone to understand, carried out some of this work in the morning room. It is also claimed that Shakespeare was so inspired by the castle that he wrote *A Midsummer Night's Dream* in 1595–6 especially for the Berkeley family.

One of the most notorious events in British history, the imprisonment and subsequent murder of Edward II in 1327, also took place at Berkeley Castle. Edward's wife, Isabella of France, plotted against him with her lover, Roger Mortimer. Edward II was imprisoned in the King's Gallery, which at the time was a much smaller

The view of the castle from the south terrace in the garden shows how it has been improved and embellished over the centuries.

room than it is today, and was brutally murdered on 21 September 1327.

In the 17th century during the Civil War, Parliamentary forces captured the castle and the wall of the keep was damaged. Curiously, an Act of Parliament was passed at the time that prohibited the repair of the breach in the keep wall, and it remains today as a dramatic reminder of that time.

INTERESTING FEATURES

✠ *The Keep*
✠ *The King's Gallery*
✠ *The Morning Room*
✠ *The Great Hall*

information

Contact details

Berkeley Castle
Berkeley
Gloucestershire
GL13 9BQ

+44 (0)1453 810332

Berkeley Castle
www.berkeley-castle.com

Transport links

Bristol Temple Meads; Bristol Parkway (then 30–35-minute taxi ride)

From Bristol/London, take the M4 and exit at junction 20; Take the M5 north to junction 14. Head north on the A38 and follow signs to Berkeley Castle

HARLECH CASTLE
Gwynedd, Wales

KEY DATES

✠ 1283 Building work begins, carried out by Master James of St George

✠ 1289 Second phase of building work is completed

✠ 1290–3 Master James of St George is constable of Harlech

✠ 1404 Welsh forces, led by Owain Glyn Dwr, gain control of Harlech

✠ 1408 Harlech is besieged by English troops

✠ 1409 Harlech is recaptured by English troops led by Prince Harry of Monmouth

✠ 1468 Castle is besieged by Yorkist troops and surrenders

✠ June 1646–March 1647 Besieged by parliamentary forces

✠ 1914 Responsibility passes to the Office of Works

✠ 1984 Cadw: Welsh Historic Monuments, takes over

✠ 1987 Becomes a World Heritage Site

Set high on a rocky crag overlooking Tremadog Bay in north Wales, Harlech Castle was designed as an impregnable and imposing English fortress able to withstand the uprisings of the Welsh people over whom it presided. With its thick walls and towering battlements, it conveys its intention of Welsh subjugation eloquently. The architect was Master James of St George, a Savoyard engineer who superintended the building of Edward I's castles in Wales. He was also constable of Harlech from 1290–3, as well as being Master of Works there.

Welsh subjugation

Edward I considered that his 'iron ring' of castles was essential if his plan to subdue and conquer north and west Wales was to succeed. Wales had originally been a collection of autonomous kingdoms, but from 1200 it became one political unit under the leadership of Llywelyn ap Iorwerth, also known as Llywelyn the Great, the ruler of Gwynedd. Llywelyn was recognized by King John, who allowed him to marry his illegitimate daughter, Joan, in 1205.

In 1267, his grandson, Llywelyn ap Gruffydd, signed a treaty recognizing Henry III as the overlord of Wales. However, he refused to pay homage to Henry's son, Edward I, when he succeeded to the English throne in 1272, thereby triggering the start of many wars between the Welsh and English.

▶ *Today the castle is still an impressive sight. It is now the responsibility of Cadw: Welsh Historic Monuments.*

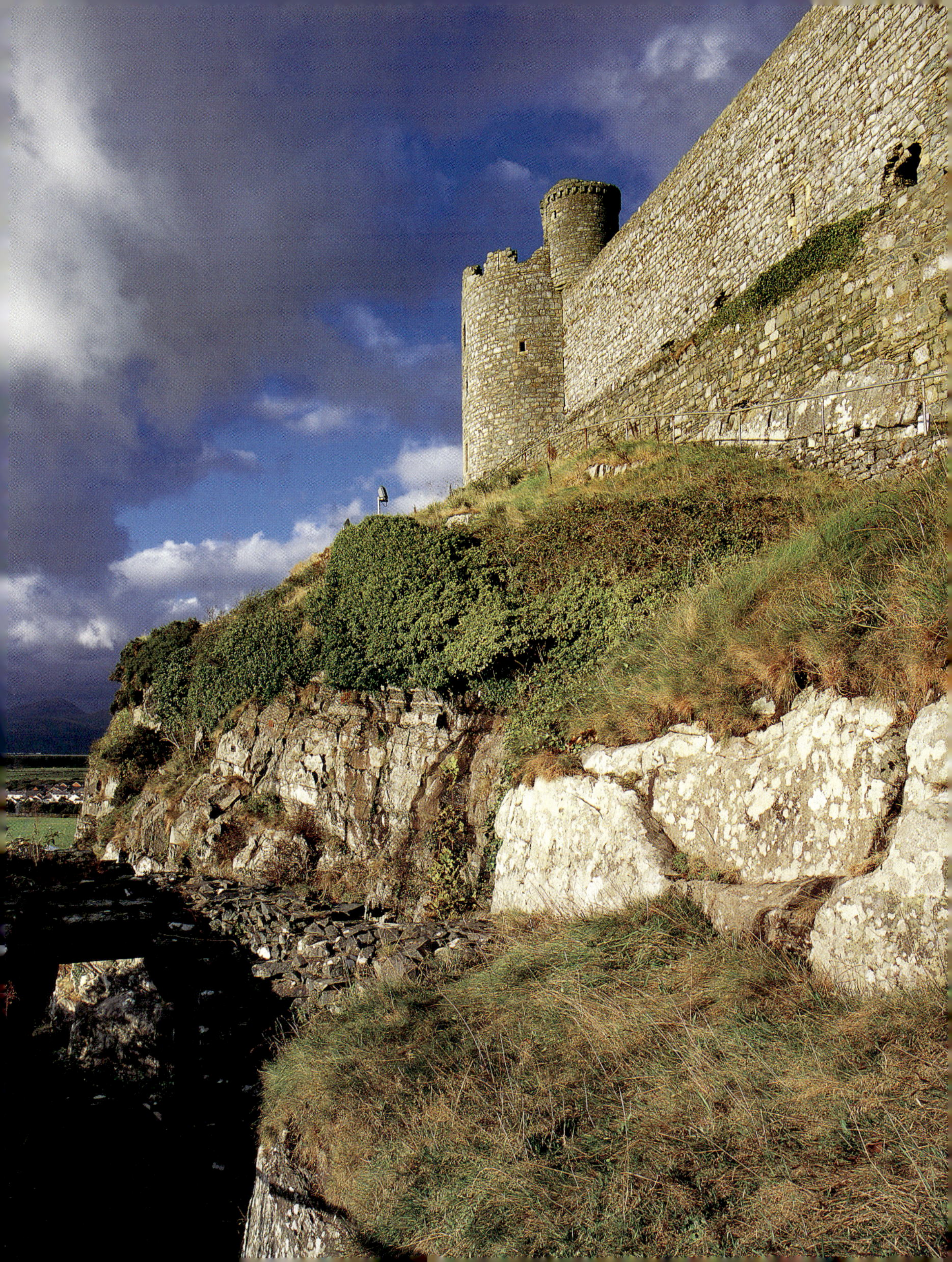

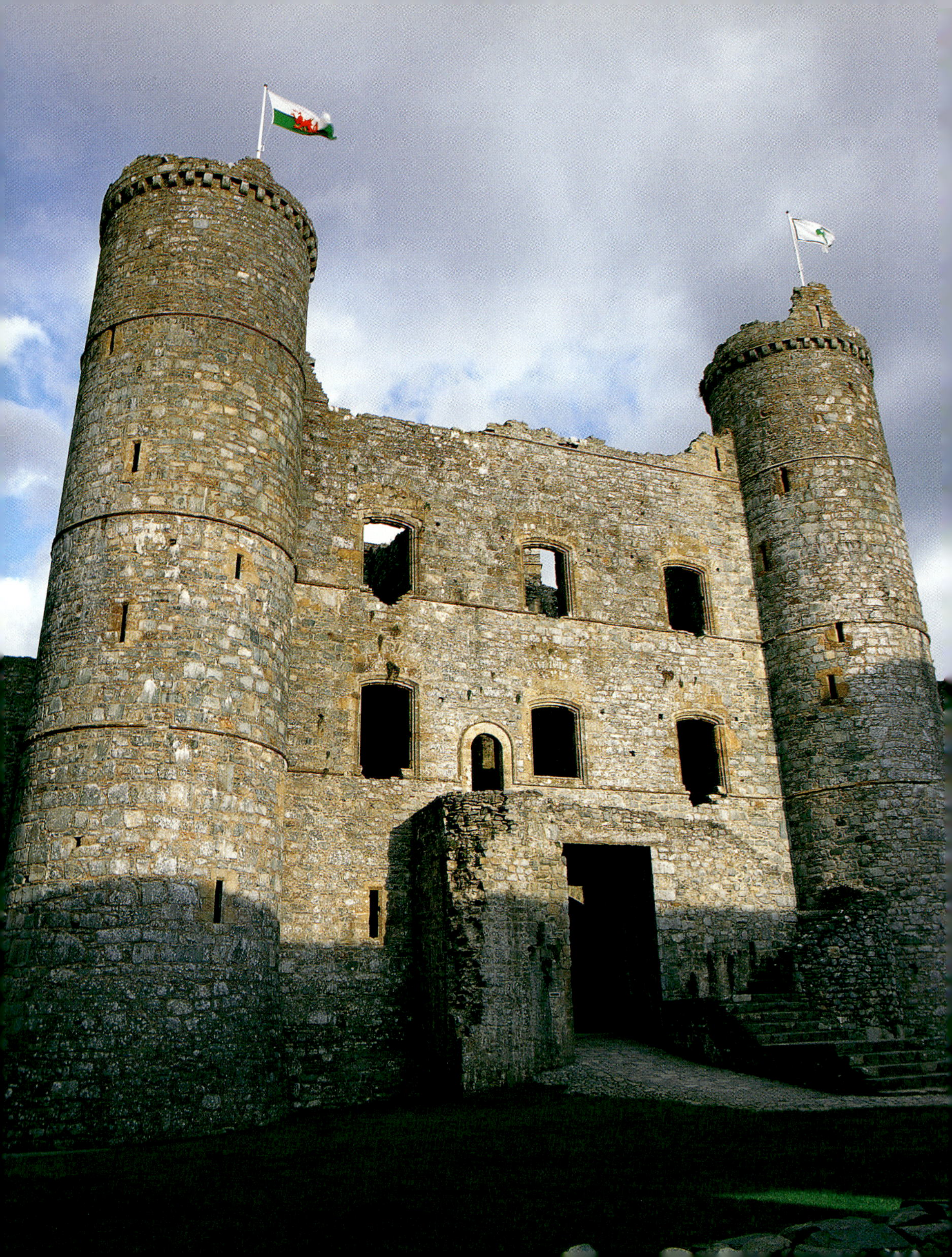

INTERESTING FEATURES

✠ The Gatehouse

✠ The main gate passage with its four arches

✠ The Inner Ward

✠ The 'Way from the Sea' stairway that leads down to the water gate

◀ *The Gatehouse leads into the Inner Ward. The six windows in the Gatehouse were all reduced in height at some point in their history.*

Strong defences

Harlech was built between 1283 and 1289 above a creek that led to the sea. The sea has since retreated, leaving Harlech stranded on a rocky prominence. At the time it was built it occupied a highly strategic position, further strengthened by the two walls that encircled it. A massive gatehouse containing three portcullises, flanked on either side by guardrooms, protected the landward side.

In 1404 Harlech faced a massive Welsh rebellion against the English, led by Owain Glyn Dwr. The Welsh won, but in 1408 it was once more under fire, this time from the English, and its outer curtain wall was severely damaged. Prince Harry of Monmouth, who later became Henry V, eventually regained the castle in early 1409.

Harlech was also involved in the Wars of the Roses between 1455 and 1485, when it was a stronghold of the Lancastrians. In 1468 it came under siege by the Yorkists, who eventually captured the castle.

During the Civil War of 1642–8, Harlech was a Royalist stronghold. It endured a siege by Parliamentary forces between June 1646 and March 1647, when it surrendered. By this time, the castle was in such a state of disrepair that its demolition was ordered, but it remained a semi-ruin until after the First World War, when the Office of Works carried out considerable repairs.

ⓘ information

Contact details

Harlech Castle
Castle Square
Harlech, Gwynedd LL46 2YH

Harlech Castle
www.harlech.com

+44 (0)1766 780552

Transport links

Harlech

CAERNARFON CASTLE
Gwynedd, North Wales

KEY DATES

✠ **1090** Robert of Rhuddlan builds a castle at Caernarfon

✠ **1283–92** First phase of building work

✠ **1294–1330** Second phase of building work

✠ **1301** Prince Edward is invested as Prince of Wales and Earl of Chester on 7 February

✠ **1403 and 1404** Caernarfon withstands sieges mounted by Owain Glyn Dwr

✠ **1646** Falls to the Parliamentarians during the Civil War

✠ **1911** Prince Edward is invested as Prince of Wales and Earl of Chester on 13 July

✠ **1969** Prince Charles is invested as Prince of Wales and Earl of Chester on 1 July

✠ **1987** Caernarfon Castle and the town walls are inscribed on the World Heritage List as an historic site of outstanding universal value

The formidable, turreted outlines of this castle dominate the skyline at Caernarfon, as they have done for the past 700 years. Caernarfon Castle occupies a prime strategic site at the point where the River Seiont flows into the Menai Strait. Despite parts of it not being completed, it is a magnificent example of a medieval fortress.

War and power in Wales

Wales was originally an independent country divided into three main areas with their own rulers: Gwynedd in north Wales, Powys in central Wales and Deheubarth in south Wales. There were many battles over power between the different rulers, who periodically also had to repel invasion from the Anglo–Saxons, Normans and Vikings. Gradually, however, the rulers of Gwynedd became most powerful and demonstrated this by calling their sons the princes of Wales. One prince, Llywelyn ap Gruffydd, later known as Llywelyn the Last, was even recognized as a prince of Wales by Henry III in 1267.

When Henry's son, Edward I, succeeded to the throne in 1272, all this changed. Edward was a powerful ruler with a genius for military strategy, and he was determined to keep the Welsh firmly under control. The first war of independence broke out between Edward I and Llywelyn in 1277, with another skirmish in 1282, during which Llywelyn was killed. Having subdued the Welsh in what had turned out to be two

▶ *The King's Gate is the main entrance to the castle. It has twin towers and demonstrates the strength of this medieval fortress.*

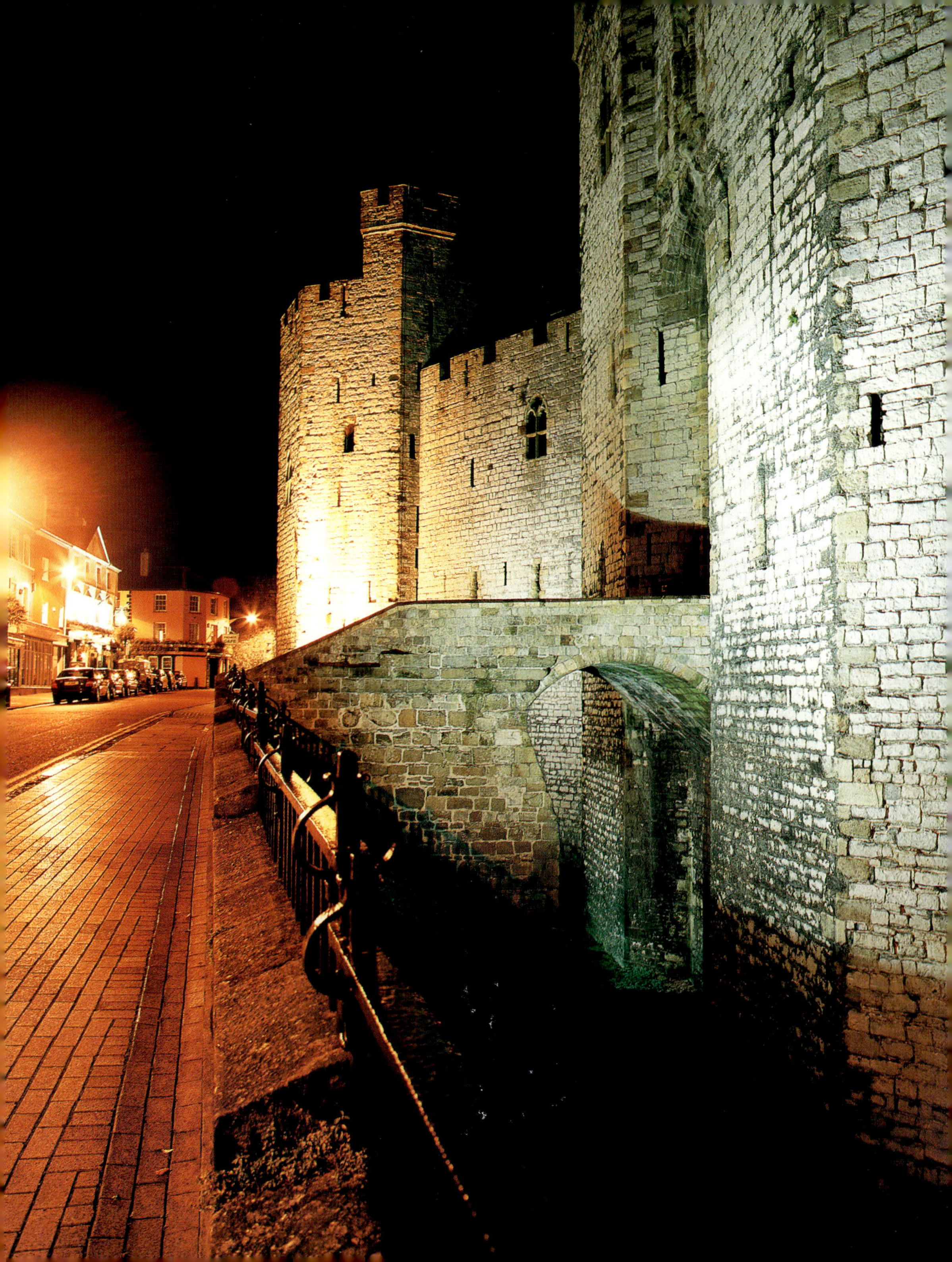

extremely costly wars, it was essential that Edward maintain the fragile status quo by repairing and strengthening the existing castles in Wales and building many more in north Wales, where the greatest threat lay.

Edward I's 'iron ring'

Edward I was returning from a crusade in 1273 when he first met Master James of St George, who later became his chief architect. James of St George had already established his credentials as a master mason, having worked on several great European castles for Count Peter II and then Philip of Savoy. One of his triumphs was St Georges d'Esperanche, which he built for Philip and from which he took his surname. Edward made an agreement with Philip that Master James should be transferred to his own service in 1278.

The combination of Edward I's money and Master James's architectural genius is one of the greatest partnerships in medieval history. Together, they created what became known as Edward I's 'iron ring' of castles in north Wales. Master James of St George was responsible, either directly or in a supervisory capacity, for all the castles built or repaired in Wales between 1276 and 1283. He built Aberystwyth, Beaumaris, Builth, Caernarfon, Chirk, Conwy, Denbigh, Flint, Harlech, Hawarden, Holt, Rhuddlan and Ruthin; and repaired Castell y Bere, Criccieth, Dolwyddelan and Hope. This extensive building programme, coming so quickly after the Welsh wars, nearly bankrupted Edward, yet he had no choice in the matter. He could afford neither the manpower nor the expense of a third war against the Welsh and, once they had been firmly put in their place, he needed to concentrate on subduing other troublesome regions of his kingdom, such as Scotland. Work began on Caernarfon Castle in 1283.

◀ *The Eagle Tower is the most imposing of all the towers at Caernarfon. At one time it contained apartments on three floors.*

134 SOUTH-WEST ENGLAND AND WALES

> ## INTERESTING FEATURES
>
> - *Statue of Edward II above the King's Gate*
> - *The King's Gate*
> - *The Queen's Gate*
> - *The Eagle Tower*
> - *The Well Tower and the well chamber within it*
> - *The town walls*

A motte and bailey castle had been built there in 1090 by Robert of Rhuddlan and its circular motte, or mound, became part of the upper ward of the new castle. To signify its importance as the English administrative centre for the region, Caernarfon was built to look different from other castles of the time. With its horizontal bands of different coloured stone and its multi-angular towers, it is believed to have been modelled on the 5th-century Roman walls at Constantinople. In common with the other castles of the time, such as Harlech and Conwy, a bastide town was also created. The castle protected the town, which in turn provided necessary supplies. Such an arrangement was popular with English settlers, which accorded well with Edward's plans.

Edward kept a close eye on the progress of the building work. He and his first wife, Eleanor of Castile, stayed on the site in July 1283 in large timber-framed apartments built specially for the purpose. Their second surviving son, Edward of Caernarfon, was born there on 25 April 1284. Their elder surviving son, Alfonso, died that August, making Edward the heir to the throne. On 7 February 1301, he was created and invested as Prince of Wales and the Earl of Chester, a move that must have angered many Welsh still chafing under the imposed rule of the English. The titles 'Prince of Wales' and 'Earl of Chester' have been bestowed together ever since.

Welsh uprising

Meanwhile, work at Caernarfon progressed, and the town was appointed the centre of government for Gwynedd, which gave it tremendous strategic and political importance. By 1292, £12,000 had been spent on the castle and town walls and all seemed to be going well until March 1294, when a massive Welsh revolt against the English caught Edward I unawares. The town walls at Caernarfon were badly damaged in September 1294, and once the mob reached the castle itself, they set light to everything they could find. By the summer of 1295, Edward had regained supremacy over the Welsh. Edward I died in 1307 and his son, Edward II, who had been the first English Prince of Wales, became king. Work at Caernarfon continued until 1330.

Saved from ruin
By the 17th century, garrisoned Welsh castles were no longer needed. Relations between the Welsh and English had improved dramatically during Tudor times, and in 1536 Henry VIII incorporated Wales into England and gave the Welsh people representation in Parliament. So Caernarfon was in a poor state of repair when it was once again pressed into service on behalf of the king during the English Civil War of 1642–8, and it fell to the Parliamentarians in 1646. Thankfully, a government order to demolish it in 1660 was ignored.

Over the centuries, Caernarfon became increasingly neglected. It was finally rescued in the last quarter of the 19th century by the deputy-constable of the time. Further repairs were carried out in readiness for an historic event that took place on 13 July 1911: the investiture of the then Prince

The Upper Ward was the setting for the investiture of Prince Charles as Prince of Wales and Earl of Chester in July 1969.

Edward (who later became Edward VIII) as Prince of Wales and Earl of Chester.

The princes of Wales

Since 1301 the title 'Prince of Wales' has been given to the eldest son of the reigning monarch; when there is no candidate for the title, it is withheld by the Crown. The current holder of the title is Prince Charles, the 21st Prince of Wales. Although given a formal investiture, the majority were invested in front of Parliament. Two notable exceptions were Edward VIII and Prince Charles, who were both invested at Caernarfon Castle using the Welsh Crown Jewels.

While Prince of Wales, Edward VIII was a glamorous, handsome prince who captured the public's imagination. He took his duties as Prince of Wales seriously, and did his best to reduce what was then a yawning gulf between royalty and the ordinary public. He was often criticized for this, as it was felt that such actions would reduce the mystique and importance of the royal family — on one occasion, he was even taken to task for carrying an umbrella as it was felt that only ordinary mortals did this. On 20 January 1936, upon the death of his father, George V, Edward succeeded to the throne. He abdicated on 11 December that year to marry Mrs Simpson.

The second investiture at Caernarfon Castle took place on 1 July 1969, when the 20-year-old Prince Charles formally received the title conferred on him in 1958 at the age of nine. The Prince had prepared for his investiture by spending a term learning Welsh at Aberystwyth University. As a reminder that relations between the English and Welsh had not always been harmonious, this investiture proved an opportunity for some Welsh Nationalists to show their displeasure with a series of bombings. However, the ceremony went ahead and was televised, combining medieval ritual with 20th-century technology.

ⓘ information

Contact details

Caernarfon Castle
8 Castle Ditch
Caernarfon, Gwynedd
LL55 2AU

+44 (0)1286 677617

Caernarfon Castle
www.caernarfon.com

Transport links

Bangor, on the Crewe–Bangor/Holyhead route

0.2 km (220 yards) Caernarfon Penllyn, route 5/5A/5B, Bangor–Caernarfon

BEAUMARIS CASTLE
Isle of Anglesey

KEY DATES

- 1295 Construction work on the castle begins
- 1330 Work stops
- 1403 The castle is taken by Owain Glyn Dwr
- 1405 The castle is recaptured by the English
- 1642 English Civil War breaks out and Beaumaris's dock becomes strategically important
- 1651 English Civil War ends
- 1925 The castle passes into state hands
- 1987 Becomes a World Heritage Site

The magnificent Beaumaris Castle is regarded as one of the finest of the great castles built under the English King Edward I in the 13th century. It was last of the 'iron ring' of castles built in north Wales (p134) and is possibly one of the most sophisticated in terms of the architecture of that time. However, it was never finished since money and supplies ran out before the fortifications could reach their intended height.

The most impressive of castles

Edward I commissioned the mason–architect Master James of St George to construct this largest and most challenging of fortified castles in north Wales at what came to be known as Beaumaris (from the Norman French 'beau mareys', meaning 'fair marsh'). Building of the handsomely designed symmetrical and concentric castle began in 1295, and a new town for English settlers was planned alongside it. St George's design involved four successive lines of fortifications encompassing the inner ward, an outer ward with an area of open ground to its exterior, a lower octagonal-shaped outer curtain, and a surrounding moat whose water came from the tidal flow of the sea. The entrance onto the sea was meant to protect the tidal dock; this allowed supply ships to sail to the castle's main gate. Invaders would have to face 14 different barriers between the curtain wall and the inner bailey, including 'murder holes', three portcullises, the door to the barbican and the barbican itself.

▲ Beaumaris is an excellent example of a concentrically designed castle with formidable defences and a large moat.

Although more than 2,500 men laboured during the summer of 1295, work slowed as the king diverted money and troops from Wales to Scotland, and stopped in 1330.

The castle was taken by the Welsh in 1403, but recaptured two years later, and then suffered from neglect. During the English Civil War, its location and dock made it key for bringing supplies and men in to aid Charles I's efforts, but it wasn't maintained after its surrender in 1646.

INTERESTING FEATURES

- *The chapel, with its ribbed stone vaulted ceiling and lancet windows*
- *The 5.5 metre (18 ft) moat*
- *The large Inner Ward*
- *The concentric design*

information

Contact details

Beaumaris Castle
Castle Street
Beaumaris Ynys Môn
LL58 8AP

Castle Wales site
www.castlewales.com
/beaumar.html

Transport links

Limited local rail services. Trains run through southern part of the islands from LLanfairpwll to Holyhead

Anglesey

BEAUMARIS CASTLE 139

Scotland

For centuries, England and Scotland were fierce adversaries, and this deeply rooted animosity is reflected in the architecture of their castles and palaces. The royal buildings in Scotland had to repel attack from enemies and foul weather alike, so they were heavily fortified with very thick walls. Many of these places have a brooding quality that is matched by the events that took place within their walls. The names of two historical figures crop up again and again, their glamour unfaded by time: Mary, Queen of Scots, who seemed hellbent on self-destruction; and Bonnie Prince Charlie, who vainly persisted in his father's lost Jacobite cause.

▶ *The sprawling mass of Edinburgh Castle towers above Princes Street Gardens and keeps watch over the city below. Each August the castle esplanade plays host to the Edinburgh Military Tattoo, which ends with a lone piper on the battlements – an important event in the annual Edinburgh International Festival.*

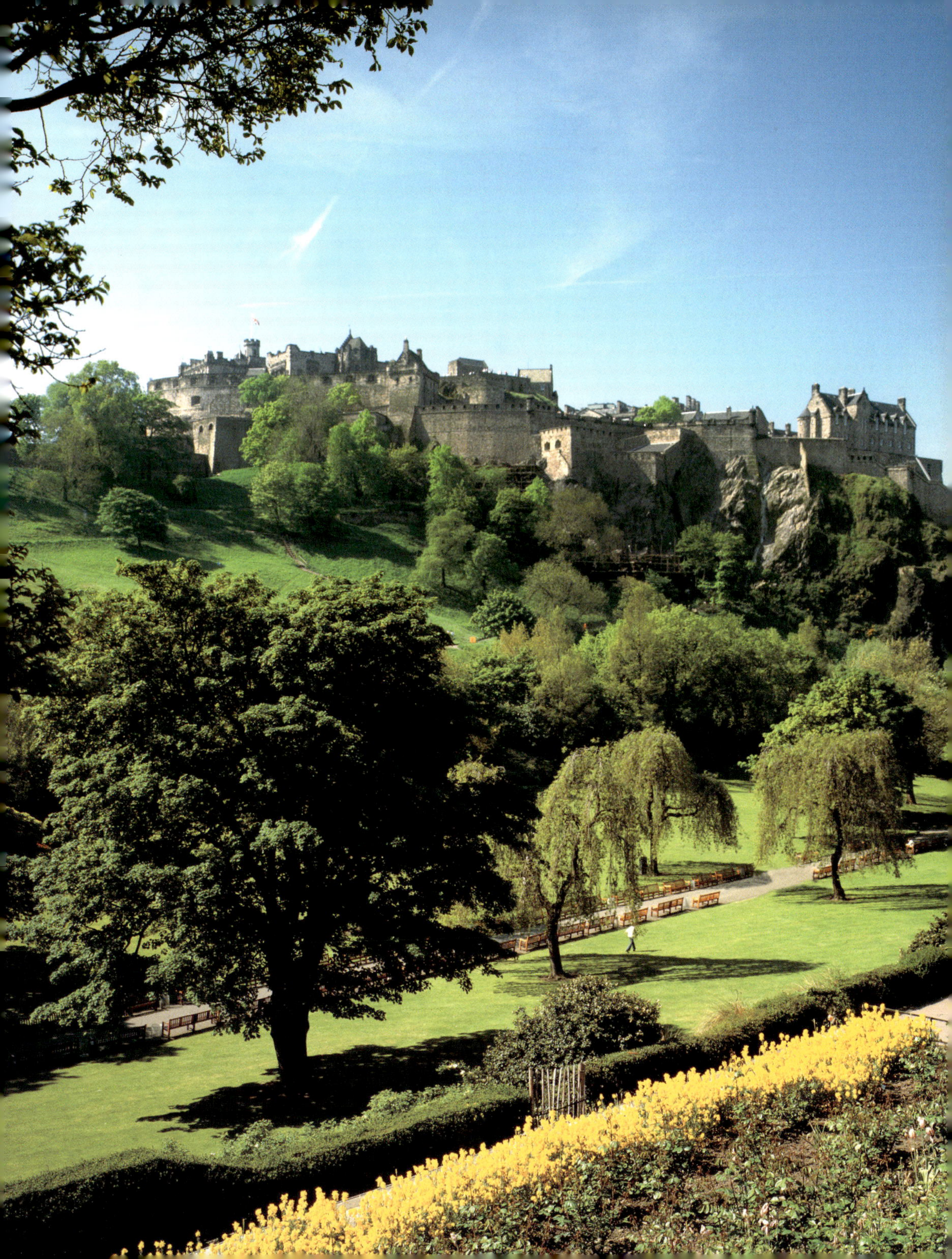

TRAQUAIR HOUSE
Innerleithen

KEY DATES

✣ *12th century The Tower is built*

✣ *1478 Traquair House is given to the Earl of Buchan, and then passed to his son, James Stuart*

✣ *1566 Mary, Queen of Scots visits Traquair during a hunting expedition*

✣ *1640s Top floor built by John Stuart, 1st Earl of Traquair*

✣ *1688 All Catholic objects are destroyed by a mob*

✣ *1745 Bonnie Prince Charlie is entertained at Traquair*

The oldest inhabited house in Scotland, Traquair House lies in a peaceful setting in the Scottish Borders. It has grown in size over the centuries as its inhabitants have built extra floors or wings, but it still has the feeling of a comfortable and much-loved family home. The Stuart family has lived at Traquair since 1478, when James III of Scotland gave the house to the Earl of Buchan, who in turn gave it to his son, James Stuart. He is an ancestor of the Maxwell Stuart family, who own Traquair today.

Royal visitors

Traquair was originally a royal hunting lodge, as the surrounding countryside was rich in deer and other wildlife and provided good sport for the royal parties. The house continued to have many royal visitors after it passed into the hands of the Stuart family, and it is claimed that 27 kings have visited Traquair. Mary, Queen of Scots, who enjoyed hunting, stayed there in 1566 with her second husband, Lord Darnley. Her prayer book and rosary can still be seen there today.

Catholic Stuarts

Although the Scottish Crown made the Stuart family lairds, they never enjoyed the wealth and luxury of some of their fellow noblemen due to their strong religious and political convictions. The family was

▶ *The exterior of Traquair, with its fairly small windows and massively thick walls, was dictated by necessity, as Scottish winters are freezing and glass was expensive.*

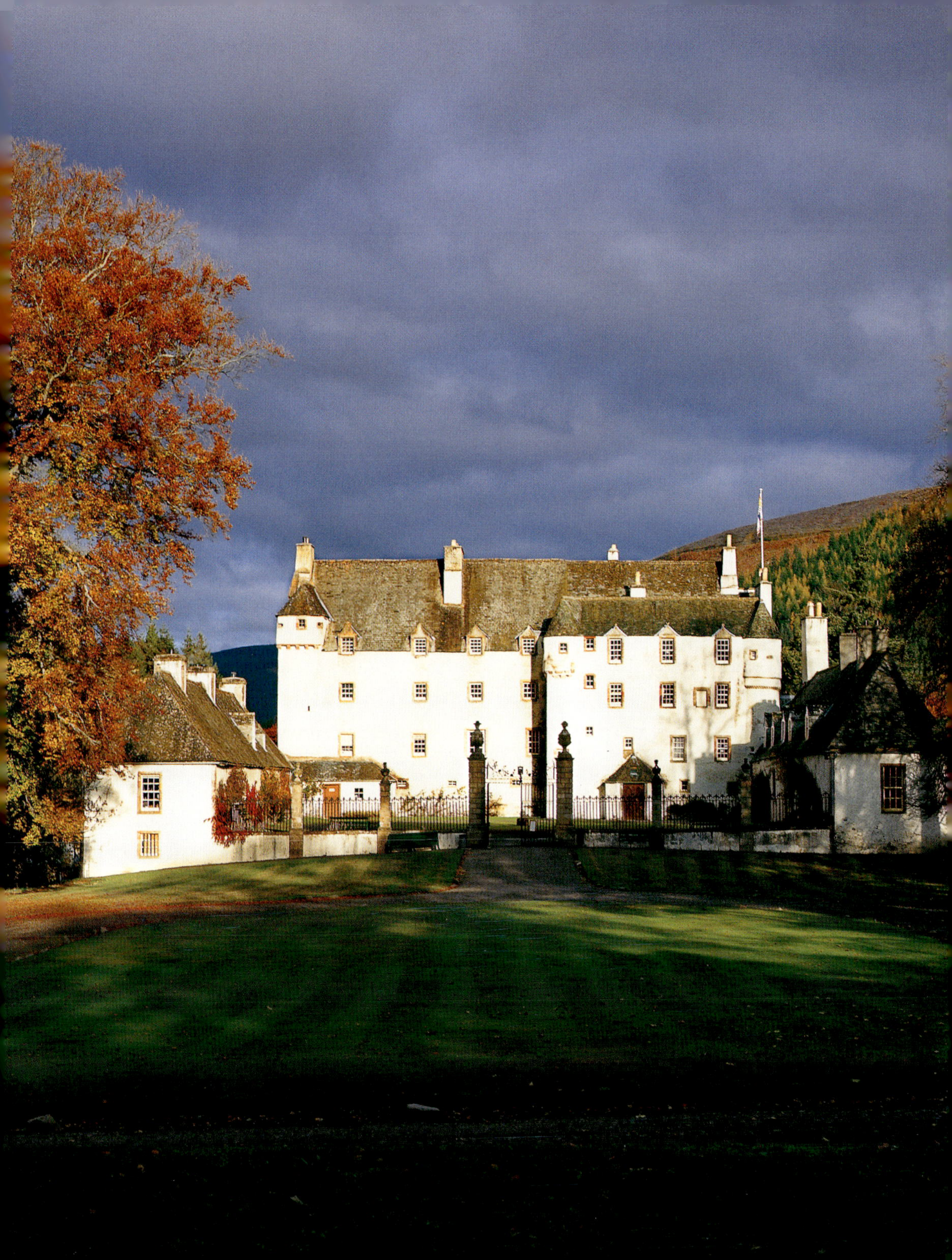

INTERESTING FEATURES

- *The museum displaying the rosary and crucifix of Mary, Queen of Scots*
- *The Bear Gates, said to have remained shut since 1745*
- *The King's Room, where Mary, Queen of Scots stayed*
- *The First Library, restored to its original 18th-century appearance*
- *The Priest's Room and its secret staircase*
- *The Brewery*
- *The gardens and walled garden*

Protestant until the 2nd Earl of Traquair converted to Catholicism in the mid-17th century, when the Catholic religion was regarded with great suspicion and fear by the state. Consequently, the Stuarts had to pay heavy taxes levied on them as recusants, or people who refused to attend the religious services established by law. Their problems were compounded after the Glorious Revolution of 1688, when James II, who had strong Catholic leanings, was forced to flee the country, leaving the throne vacant for his Protestant daughter and son-in-law, Mary II and William III.

Jacobite sympathies

Supporters of the deposed James II, and later of his exiled son and grandson, known as the Old Pretender and Bonnie Prince Charlie respectively, were known as Jacobites and considered to be profoundly dangerous subversives. The Stuarts fell into

▶ Mary, Queen of Scots stayed in the King's Room in 1566. It is particularly memorable for the ornate decorations on the four-poster bed.

this category and in 1688 a Protestant mob from Peebles ransacked Traquair, smashing every religious object they could find. The Jacobite sympathies of the 4th Earl landed him in prison in Edinburgh Castle during the 1715 Rising for the Old Pretender, and his son, the 5th Earl, spent two years in the Tower of London after taking part in the 1745 Rising of Bonnie Prince Charlie. It is said that the 5th Earl entertained Bonnie Prince Charlie at Traquair. After he left, the 5th Earl locked the Bear Gates to Traquair and swore they would remain shut until a Stuart king was again crowned in London.

The combination of being Catholic and Jacobite meant the Stuarts could not afford many additions or improvements to Traquair from 1700 onwards, so the house is full of wonderful period details and furnishings.

ⓘ information

Contact details

Traquair House
Innerleithen
Peeblesshire EH44 6PW

☎ +44 (0)1896 830323

🌐 Traquair House
www.traquair.co.uk

Transport links

🚆 Edinburgh Waverley Station
(about 1-hour drive)

🚌 62 to Innerleithen from
St Andrews Bus Station,
Edinburgh

TRAQUAIR HOUSE

EDINBURGH CASTLE
Edinburgh

KEY DATES

✠ *1093 Queen Margaret dies in the Castle of Maidens on 16 November*

✠ *1296 Edward I captures the castle and steals the treasures*

✠ *1341 The Scots regain the castle*

✠ *1566 The future James VI is born in the castle on 19 June*

✠ *1615–17 Royal palace rebuilt in honour of James VI of Scotland and I of England*

✠ *1818 Sir Walter Scott finds the Honours of Scotland*

✠ *1846 St Margaret's Chapel is rediscovered and restored*

✠ *1996 Stone of Destiny is returned to the castle on 30 November*

Contemporary Edinburgh is a vibrant, busy city that deservedly attracts visitors from all over the world. There are modern shopping centres and the new Scottish Parliament building, symbolizing Scotland's new-found independence, now stands at the end of the Royal Mile. Yet there are many reminders of ancient Edinburgh, from the claustrophobic, winding streets of the Old Town to the medieval Palace of Holyroodhouse, scene of one of the most notorious murders in Scottish history. Until the 18th century, what is now Princes Street Gardens was an uninviting, stinking stretch of water known as Nor' Loch, into which the city's waste and rubbish were thrown. Go back 1,000 years earlier and the two tallest points in Edinburgh were Arthur's Seat, all that remains of a 340-million-year-old volcano, and irregular outcrops of the rock formed by ice sheets in the last Ice Age.

Battles with the English

This is the Edinburgh that King Malcolm III and Queen Margaret would have known in the 11th century. Even then there was a royal palace, called the Castle of Maidens, on the castle rock. Although Malcolm acknowledged William the Conqueror as his overlord, this did not prevent William from invading northern England five times. On the fifth occasion, in November 1093, Malcolm was killed in battle at Alnwick. When his wife heard the news, she took

▶ *At night, the illuminated buildings of Edinburgh Castle dominate the skyline.*

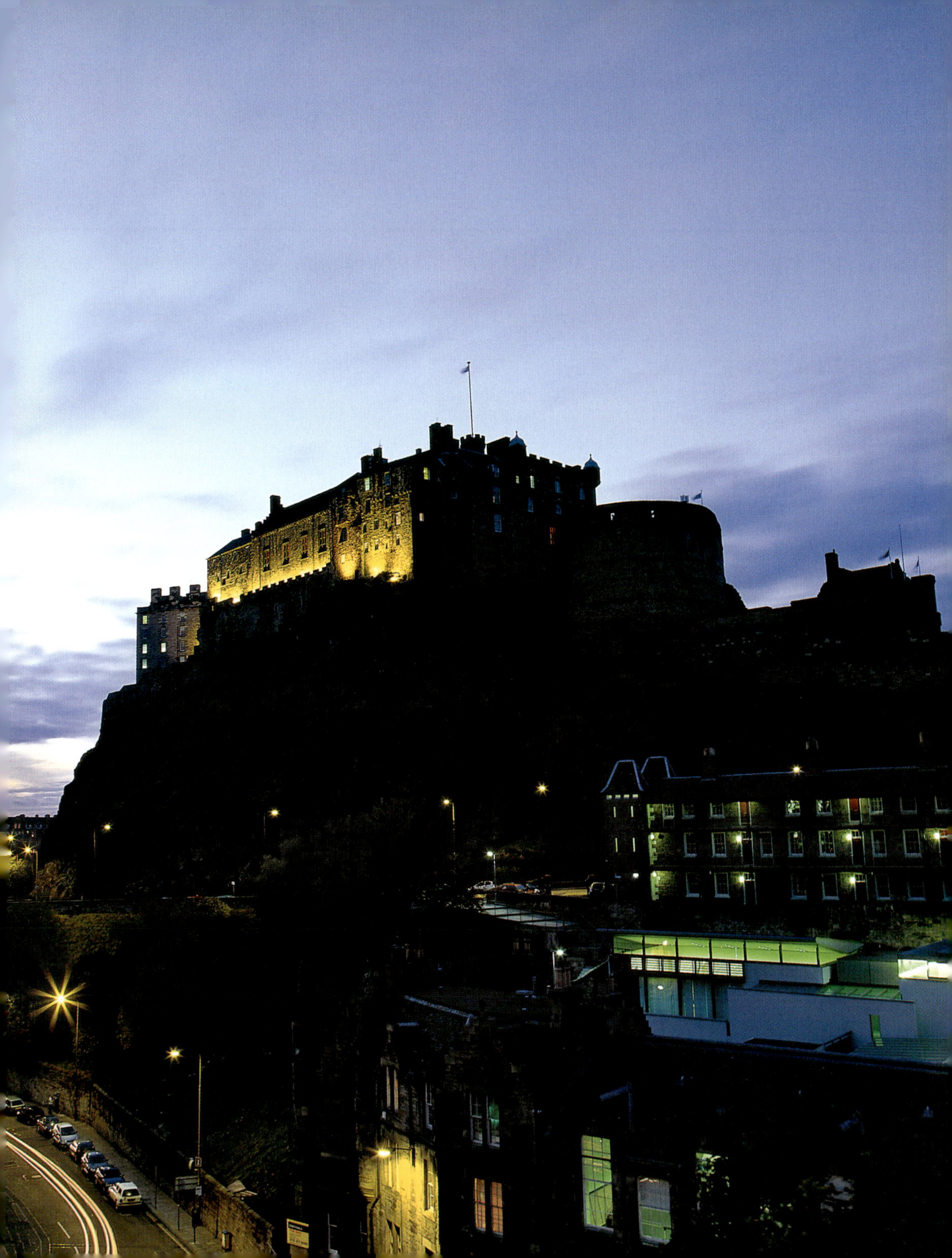

INTERESTING FEATURES

- ✠ The National War Museum of Scotland, the Royal Scots Regimental Museum and the Royal Scots Dragoon Guards Regimental Museum in the Middle Ward
- ✠ Mons Meg in the Upper Ward
- ✠ St Margaret's Chapel in the Upper Ward
- ✠ The Scottish National War Memorial in Crown Square
- ✠ The Honours of Scotland and the Stone of Destiny in the Crown Room
- ✠ The Birthchamber in the Royal Palace
- ✠ The ceiling and frieze in the Laich Hall in the Royal Palace

to her bed and died a couple of days later. Four of their sons became kings of Scotland, but it was the youngest, David I, who turned the castle into an important royal palace. Among the buildings erected in his reign was St Margaret's Chapel, dedicated to his mother's memory, which is the oldest building in Edinburgh.

Much of the castle was built of timber, and so was not strong enough to withstand the assault mounted on it by Edward I in 1296 in the opening salvos of the Wars of Independence between the English and Scots. This began a 45-year period in which

◀ The apsidal chancel (left) in St Margaret's Chapel is separated by an arch from the rectangular nave.

▶ The king spied on courtiers through an opening to the right of the fireplace in the Great Hall (right).

the English and Scots fought for ownership of the castle, recapturing it by turns until it was wrenched from the English for the last time in 1341. By this time, the castle was uninhabitable, having been dismantled on the orders of Robert the Bruce in 1314 to stop it being used against him by the English; his son, David II, had to rebuild the place. He built David's Tower, which now lies in ruins beneath the Half-Moon Battery, although parts of it are accessible.

Crown Square
James III (r. 1460–88) spent a large part of his reign at Edinburgh Castle, during which time he oversaw a great deal of building work. This included work on the royal palace that stood on the east side of the main courtyard of the castle, today called Crown Square. This courtyard housed the most important buildings in the castle: the Royal Palace, the Great Hall, the Royal Gunhouse and St Mary's Church – unfortunately the latter two buildings

no longer exist. Two stone cellars, known as the Castle Vaults, lie beneath Crown Square. These vaults have performed a variety of functions over the centuries, such as providing storage for food and munitions and as military prisons, most notably for prisoners of war in the Napoleonic Wars at the turn of the 19th century.

The united crown
The exposed position of Edinburgh Castle made it a cold and inhospitable place. After the reign of James III, succeeding Scottish monarchs preferred the comfort of Holyroodhouse (pp152–61) at the other end of the Royal Mile. In the spring of 1566, Mary, Queen of Scots was forced to take refuge in the Royal Palace in the castle, as her political and personal lives were in crisis and she feared for her unborn child. This child was delivered in the Birthchamber on 19 June, and grew up to become James VI of Scotland and I of England, uniting the crowns of two countries that had periodically been at war for centuries.

Mary was forced to abdicate her throne 13 months later and her infant son, James VI, became king. Mary had a loyal supporter in Sir William Kirkcaldy of Grange, the governor of the castle, and in 1571 he was involved in a protracted siege (known as the 'lang siege') against the regent ruling on behalf of the infant James. This siege ended in 1573 when Elizabeth I sent enough guns to ensure victory over the occupants of the castle. Sir William was executed in public.

James's succession to the English throne in 1603 unwittingly hastened the end of the castle's life as a royal residence, despite the fact that the Royal Palace was rebuilt during his reign. James might have been king of both England and Scotland, but the former was generally considered to be the more important country and it was also the seat of government. When James's son, Charles I,

◀ The Laich Hall on the ground floor of the Royal Palace was created for a visit in 1617 by James VI of Scotland and I of England.

▶ *The vaults beneath Crown Square have been used for storage of food and ordnance, and were also home to prisoners of war.*

slept in the castle on the night before his Scottish coronation in June 1633, he was the last reigning monarch to do so. Charles was executed in 1649 and Britain became a republic. The crown passed to his son, Charles II, who was in exile in France at the time but was eventually crowned at Scone Abbey on 1 January 1651. Such strong Scottish support for the exiled king had alerted Oliver Cromwell, who lost no time in setting up a powerful garrison in the castle. The army was permanently stationed here, and the defences strengthened.

The one o'clock gun

Edinburgh Castle once again came under fire at the start of the 18th century, during the five Jacobite Risings in support of the exiled James Francis Edward Stuart, known as the 'Old Pretender'. A Jacobite attempt to capture the castle nearly succeeded in 1715 but failed due to a quirky combination of circumstances. After the 1745 Rising led by the Old Pretender's son, Bonnie Prince Charlie, the castle's function as a defensive fortress has never again been put to the test. Nevertheless, a gun – the one o'clock gun – is still fired from the battlements in the Middle Ward each Monday to Saturday.

ⓘ information

Contact details

Edinburgh Castle
Castlehill
Edinburgh
EH1 2NG

Edinburgh Castle
www.edinburghcastle.gov.uk

☎ +44 (0)131 225 9846

Transport links

Edinburgh Waverley

St Andrews Station, Edinburgh

EDINBURGH CASTLE

THE PALACE OF HOLYROODHOUSE
Edinburgh

KEY DATES

- 1528–32 James V builds the Northwest Tower
- 1535–6 James V builds a new West Front for the palace
- 1565 Mary, Queen of Scots marries Lord Darnley at Holyroodhouse on 29 July
- 1566 David Rizzio murdered in Mary, Queen of Scots' apartments on 9 March
- 1567 Mary marries the 4th Earl of Bothwell at Holyroodhouse on 15 May
- 1633 Charles I crowned at Holyrood Abbey in June
- 1745 Bonnie Prince Charlie briefly holds court at Holyroodhouse
- 1850 Queen Victoria visits Holyroodhouse in August
- 1911 State visit of George V and Queen Mary
- 2002 The Queen's Gallery opens

Two royal palaces in Edinburgh lie a mile apart from each other, linked by the Royal Mile that snakes its way through the most ancient part of the city. Edinburgh Castle keeps watch from its perch on the craggy outcrop Castle Rock, while the Palace of Holyroodhouse sits beneath the looming bulk of Arthur's Seat and Salisbury Crags. The two palaces could not be more different in appearance or atmosphere, and it is little wonder that Scottish monarchs throughout the centuries have preferred to live in the picturesque environs of Holyroodhouse rather than in the draughty setting of Edinburgh Castle.

Monastic beginnings

What we know now as Holyroodhouse began life as an Augustinian monastery, the Abbey of Holyrood, founded by King David I in 1128. Holyrood means 'holy cross', and the abbey's most important relic was a piece of the True Cross that David's mother, who was canonized in the 13th century as St Margaret, brought to Scotland. Legend has it that while out hunting, David had a vision of a stag with a cross between its antlers, so he founded his monastery on that very spot.

Such an important abbey needed a guesthouse, and this eventually developed into the palace that we know today. Nothing remains of the early buildings, including

▶ *James V's 16th-century tower stands to the left of the west front of the palace. It is matched on the right by the tower built over a century later in 1671.*

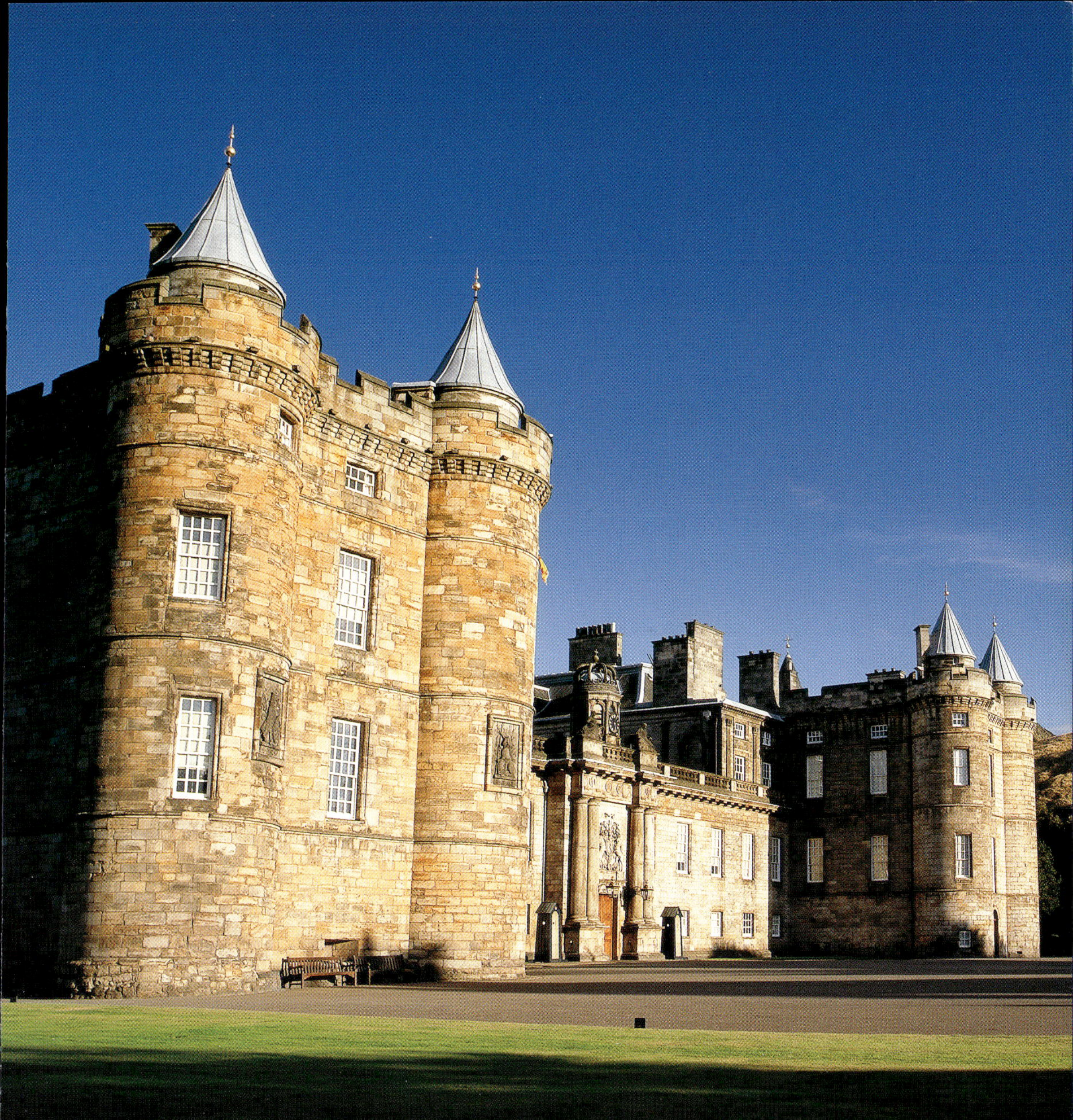

the gatehouse built by James IV in preparation for his dynastically important marriage to Margaret Tudor, daughter of Henry VII, in the abbey on 8 August 1503. Both kings were anxious to create greater harmony between their two countries, as the many wars waged between them were expensive, time-consuming and troublesome. Their efforts were in vain, as James IV died in battle against his brother-in-law, Henry VIII, at Flodden Field on 9 September 1513.

James V

A family pattern repeated itself with each Stewart monarch from James I to James VI; each succeeded to the throne at a very early

> ## INTERESTING FEATURES
>
> ✠ *The 110 portraits of the kings of Scotland in the Great Gallery*
>
> ✠ *The plasterwork ceiling above the Great Stair*
>
> ✠ *The ceiling of the Evening Drawing Room*
>
> ✠ *The King's Bedchamber*
>
> ✠ *Mary, Queen of Scots' Supper Room*

age, sometimes when only a few days old. When James IV died on 9 September 1513, his 17-month-old son was crowned James V. James was to have a very important impact on the history of Holyroodhouse, not only because of the building work he carried out but also because the story of his daughter, Mary, Queen of Scots, is tightly interwoven with that of Holyroodhouse.

Between 1528 and 1532, James V built an enormous tower to house the royal apartments. More building work followed between 1535 and 1536, with a new, highly decorative west front. In constructing this, James followed his father's example of making the palace more habitable for his future bride, Madeleine Valois. She was the daughter of Francis I of France and, despite being in poor health, represented another important dynastic link between Scotland and other countries. Whereas there had

◀ *The grisaille frieze in the Queen's Bedchamber is said to have been created for the visit of James VI of Scotland and I of England in 1617.*

always been an uneasiness between Scotland and England, there was greater understanding between Scotland and France: this was, after all, known as the 'auld alliance', after the anti-English alliance made between the two countries in 1295.

Sadly, the sickly Madeleine had barely arrived at Holyroodhouse before she died in July 1537 and was buried in the abbey. Anxious to maintain his friendly links with France, James quickly contracted another French marriage, this time to Mary of Guise, the widow of Louis II, the Duc de Longueville. They married in 1538 and Mary was crowned Queen Consort in the abbey in February 1540. Although they had three children, only their daughter, Mary, survived infancy.

Mary, Queen of Scots

Mary was six days old when she became queen on 14 December 1542, and just under nine months old when she was crowned on 9 September 1543. In the 16th century,

THE PALACE OF HOLYROODHOUSE 155

the children of monarchs were generally treated as pawns in a game of power, dynastic alliance and strategy; Mary was no exception. Half-French through her mother, Mary of Guise, she was married to the young French Dauphin in April 1558 in Paris and became Queen Consort after the death of her father-in-law, Henry II, in September 1559. Her husband, Francis II, died in December of the following year, and Mary returned to Scotland. However, the religious landscape of the country had altered dramatically, having switched from Catholicism, which she practised, to staunch Protestantism under the zealous, provocative and extremist leadership of John Knox.

Romantic folly and dangerous plots

After the death of her first husband, it was important that Mary should remarry and, being so eligible, she held the ultimate trump card. This was a source of worry to her cousin, Elizabeth I, who feared that Mary would marry into one of the great European Catholic royal families, thereby creating a powerful alliance against her.

She need not have worried; Mary became enchanted by Henry Stuart, Lord Darnley. He was tall and handsome, and she was unable to resist him. As he was her step-cousin – they shared the same grandmother, Margaret Tudor – they had to apply for a papal dispensation to marry. Mary's advisers were against the marriage, but this only fuelled her desire to go through with it. In fact, they were in such a hurry to get married that their wedding took place on 29 July 1565 in the chapel of Holyroodhouse, before the dispensation arrived.

When Mary, who was still only 23, married Darnley, she hoped that he would protect, support and guide her. She soon realized, however, that there was little chance of this, as he was self-serving, jealous and vain. Shortly before their marriage, Mary had bestowed on Darnley the title 'King of this our Kingdom', and he was called King Henry by the Scots people. This new status was not enough to satisfy Darnley: he wanted the Crown Matrimonial that would give him equal powers to those of Mary and the right of succession if Mary died before she had children. He also wanted the glory and power without the duties; he was often to be found out hunting and hawking while Mary attended to affairs of state. Relations soon became strained between Darnley and Mary, now pregnant. She increasingly sought the company of her secretary, David Rizzio, leading to gossip that they were lovers.

In addition to her marital troubles, Mary was having difficulties with some Protestant lords of Scotland who were rebelling against her. Matters came to a head in March 1566, when the lords conspired with other interested parties,

▲ The King's Bedchamber lies at the centre of the palace. The overmantel painting is by Jacob de Wet the Younger, who also painted all the portraits in the Great Gallery.

including Darnley, to ensure their return from exile, the upholding of the Protestant religion and the Crown Matrimonial for Darnley. Mary and Rizzio chose to ignore the rumours that something terrible was about to happen.

Murder and fear

On the night of 9 March 1566, Mary held an informal and intimate supper party in her apartments on the second floor of the palace. Darnley's apartments were on the floor below, and were linked to Mary's by

THE PALACE OF HOLYROODHOUSE 157

The walls of the palace and abbey are rich in magnificent architectural detail.

a narrow staircase. (This privy staircase is now hidden behind the Charles II panelling.) Darnley and his fellow conspirators burst into Mary's supper room, dragged Rizzio across her bedchamber and into the doorway of the adjoining outer chamber. There he was frenziedly stabbed between 50 and 60 times and left to die.

Mary realized that her own life was in danger and moved to Edinburgh Castle in preparation for the birth of her son, who later became James VI, in June 1566. She was now emotionally involved with James, 4th Earl of Bothwell, who was the sheriff of Edinburgh, but she still needed to deal with Darnley. There were alarming rumours that he planned to seize the baby prince, who at that time was at Stirling Castle, so mother and baby were reunited at Holyroodhouse in January 1567. Darnley, who had been ill in Glasgow, was brought back to Edinburgh. Mary wanted him where she could keep an eye on him, so Darnley was installed in an old house called Kirk o' Field, a short distance from Holyroodhouse.

In the early hours of 10 February 1567, an explosion split the air: Kirk o' Field lay in ruins, having been blown up, probably by Bothwell. Darnley's body was found in the garden and taken to Holyroodhouse, where it lay in state for several days before being buried in the Chapel Royal.

Mary's final years

Without realizing it, Mary was playing out the final scenes of her life in Scotland. She appeared to be ricocheting from one unwise decision to the next, and she now agreed, under duress, to marry Bothwell. The wedding took place in the Great Hall at Holyroodhouse on 15 May 1567, only three months after Darnley's death. Both the Pope and Protestant Scotland were outraged by this marriage, and Mary was forced to abdicate in favour of her son on 24 July. She and her followers crossed into England, where she was captured and held as a prisoner by her cousin, Elizabeth I, for 18 years before her execution for treason on 8 February 1587.

Decline and rebuilding

Following true Stewart tradition, Mary's baby son became James VI at the age of 13 months. He succeeded to the English throne as James I following the death of his cousin, Elizabeth I, on 24 March 1603, thus uniting the warring countries of England and Scotland under a single crown. James was now expected to rule his kingdom from England and so Holyroodhouse inevitably fell into decline.

The state of the palace became even more parlous during the Civil War, when Cromwell's English troops badly damaged much of it. When Charles II was restored to the throne in 1660, he was determined that Holyroodhouse should be repaired. Work started in 1671, directed by James Maitland, 1st Duke of Lauderdale, who was then Secretary of State for Scotland. The results were a masterpiece of baroque architecture, combining an elegance and sophistication that were unknown in Scotland at that time. James V's tower was duplicated at the other end of the west front and new royal apartments were built around a beautiful quadrangle, whose cloisters referred back to the original Augustinian monastery. The old west front was rebuilt and the windows of James V's tower were stripped of their ancient iron grilles and given sash windows.

The interior of the palace was no less stunning, with magnificent plastered ceilings and many decorative paintings. The final grand flourish was delivered by the Dutch painter, Jacob de Wet the Younger, who was commissioned by Charles II to paint a sequence of portraits of the kings of Scotland for the Great Gallery.

Catholic conversion

Charles's brother James, Duke of York, moved into Holyroodhouse in 1679. He had strong Catholic sympathies, which ran counter to the mood of the times and eventually cost him the throne when he became James II of England and VII of

▲ *Today, beautiful Holyroodhouse, the former seat of a long line of Scottish monarchs, stands next to the Scottish Parliament building, the symbol of Scottish Independence.*

Scotland. He ordered the abbey church to be equipped for Catholic services, but the work was still in progress when he was forced to abdicate in December 1688. William of Orange, James's Dutch Protestant son-in-law, was invited to take over the throne, and when news reached Edinburgh that he had finally landed in Devon, a mob descended on Holyroodhouse and destroyed every item they could find with a Catholic connection.

Bonnie Prince Charlie

Holyroodhouse became a lavish home for officers of state, who lived in luxury in the grace-and-favour apartments that were assigned to them. It had a brief renaissance as a palace in 1745 during

Bonnie Prince Charlie's doomed attempt to capture the throne for his father, the son of James II of England and VII of Scotland. The charismatic and romantic young prince held a glittering court at Holyroodhouse for five weeks in the autumn of 1745, but this was the final flowering of his Jacobite cause, as he was eventually defeated at the Battle of Culloden in April 1746. Nevertheless, the cult of the Jacobites was considered to be so dangerous to national security that the wearing of Highland dress was banned.

Rescued again from ruin

The gradual decline of Holyroodhouse continued, and when the roof of the abbey church collapsed in 1768, it was left as a ruin. However, the palace slowly became an important venue on the 18th-century tourist trail, thanks to its vivid connections with Mary, Queen of Scots.

The palace once again fulfilled its royal role in 1822, when George IV made a state visit to Scotland, although Holyroodhouse was in such a sad and tatty state that he slept elsewhere, and only visited the palace for the state occasions that took place there.

As with so many other royal palaces that had been allowed to fade into gentle obscurity, Holyroodhouse was rescued and renovated by Queen Victoria. She enjoyed a lifelong love affair with Scotland and was profoundly moved when she first visited the palace in 1850. Despite the palace's importance as an historic monument, Holyroodhouse still languished in a rather poor state of repair.

During the 20th century, the importance and beauty of Holyroodhouse were finally recognized, and it was sympathetically modernized and restored. Today, it is the official Scottish residence of the Queen, where she holds important state functions such as investitures, garden parties and summits. It is also the point where ancient converges with modern: the new Scottish Parliament building, a 21st-century symbol of Scottish Independence, stands next to the old Holyroodhouse, once the seat of a long line of Scottish monarchs.

information

Contact details

Palace of Holyrood
Canongate
The Royal Mile
EH8 8DX

+44 (0)131 524 1120

Royal Collection
www.royalcollection.org.uk/default.asp?action=article&ID=36

Transport links

Edinburgh Waverley

St Andrews Station, Edinburgh

LINLITHGOW PALACE
Linlithgow

KEY DATES

- 1301–3 Original royal manor house is fortified by Edward I
- 1425–37 Work carried out on Linlithgow Palace
- 1461 The fugitive Henry VI of England stays at the palace
- 1488–1513 Building work is carried out by James IV
- 1512 Prince James (James V) is born at the palace in April
- 1542 Princess Mary (later Mary, Queen of Scots) is born at the palace on 8 December
- 1551–60 The palace is assigned to Mary of Guise as her personal residence
- 1633 Charles I visits
- 1663 The Cromwellian fortifications are demolished
- 1745 Bonnie Prince Charlie stays in the palace
- 1746 The palace is ruined by fire on February 1
- 1906 The fireplace in the Great Hall is restored

Despite its ruined condition, Linlithgow Palace is considered to be one of the most atmospheric and photogenic royal residences in Britain. It sits serenely on a promontory in Linlithgow Loch with the tower of St Michael's Church rising next to it. The history of the palace is evocative, running through several centuries, until it was severely damaged by English troops in 1746 after they had succeeded in subduing the supporters of the Jacobite pretender, Bonnie Prince Charlie.

Sporadic building works

A royal manor house originally stood on the site now occupied by the palace; it burnt down in 1424 in a fire that also destroyed most of the town. James I of Scotland, who had only just been released from prolonged captivity in England, began to build the palace in 1425. The building work went so well that by 1428 he was even able to spend a few days here. Money was no object and the rooms were decorated in the latest fashions. Work was temporarily suspended after James's assassination in 1437, and his successor, James II, had little involvement in the project before his own untimely death in 1460. Nevertheless, the palace must have been in a habitable state at this time because the young James III used it as a residence and gave it to his wife, Margaret of Denmark, as a wedding present in 1469.

▶ *The West Range was completed by James IV and contained the royal apartments for James and his wife, Margaret Tudor.*

LINLITHGOW PALACE

INTERESTING FEATURES

✠ *James's insignia on the outer gateway*

✠ *The Great Hall*

✠ *The North Range*

✠ *The fountain in the courtyard*

✠ *The King's Presence Chamber*

✠ *The Chapel Royal*

The lives of these Stewart monarchs were marked by tragedy, which struck yet again when James III was assassinated in 1488. His 15-year-old son, James IV, inherited Linlithgow Palace and immediately began developing it into a comfortable, modern residence. One of his greatest contributions was to create the West Range, containing new royal apartments, which transformed Linlithgow into a four-sided building with a central quadrangle. The palace was also fortified, although on a rudimentary scale, with a barbican built on to the east wall. When James died at the Battle of Flodden Field on 9 September 1513, work at the palace was virtually complete.

James V was born at the palace in April 1512 and succeeded to the throne as a baby. His birthplace was neglected for several years until more work began on it in 1534. Like his father, James V remodelled various areas of the palace, and he moved the main entrance from the east side to the south of the building. He also built an outer gateway, which is still decorated with insignia from the four orders of chivalry to which he belonged: the English Garter, the Scottish Thistle, the Burgundian Golden Fleece and the French St Michael.

Fortification and destruction

Princess Mary, who was later to become Mary, Queen of Scots, was born at Linlithgow Palace on 8 December 1542, and her father, James V, died at Falkland Palace six days later. At the age of seven months, Mary was moved to the safety of Stirling Castle, and did not set foot in Linlithgow for another 20 years.

When Mary's son, James VI of Scotland, also became James I of England in 1603, it was the beginning of a long period of neglect for many Scottish palaces and castles because the court moved down to reside in England. The North Range of Linlithgow fell down in 1607, and work on replacing it did not begin until 1618. Linlithgow Palace was again repaired in 1633 for a visit from

▲ Although it is now roofless, the Great Hall in the East Range of Linlithgow Palace is one of the finest medieval halls in existence.

Charles I, and it was then fortified by Oliver Cromwell's troops when Cromwell stayed there during the winter of 1650. After English soldiers destroyed Linlithgow Palace in 1746, whether by accident or design, it was left in its ruined state.

Plans to turn it into a museum or law courts were mooted in the 1890s, but these came to nothing, and today Linlithgow is left as a fine reminder of the turbulent Stewart reign in Scotland.

information

Contact details

Linlithgow Palace
Kirkgate, Linlithgow
EH49 7AL

+44 (0)131 668 8800

Historic Scotland
www.historic-scotland.gov.uk/propertyoverview?PropID=pl_199&PropName=Linlithgow%20Palace

Transport links

Linlithgow

LINLITHGOW PALACE

STIRLING CASTLE
Stirling

KEY DATES

- c.1107–15 Alexander I has a castle chapel dedicated and endowed
- 1296 Edward I seizes the castle
- 1297 Battle of Stirling Bridge on 11 September
- 1314 Battle of Bannockburn on 24 June
- c.1500 James IV begins work on the new castle
- 1538 James V marries Mary of Guise and begins work on the palace
- 1708–14 Stirling's defences strengthened
- 1794 The Duke of Argyll's Highland regiment musters at the castle
- 1849 Queen Victoria visits the castle
- 1855 The King's Old Building is damaged by fire
- 1906 Care of the castle is transferred from the War Office to the Office of Works

Should any visitor to Stirling Castle need to be reminded of one of the most important episodes in its long history and that of Scotland, they have only to look north to the Wallace Monument that towers over the trees on Abbey Craig. This monument was erected in honour of William Wallace, who led the Scottish army to victory against the English at the Battle of Stirling Bridge in 1297. A statue of Wallace stands on a plinth on the monument, forever surveying the land that he protected.

Wallace would not recognize the castle that stands here today, as the present castle was built in the 15th century. The original castle was made from timber and has long since disappeared. We do not know when the first castle was built, but it had already been established by the beginning of the 1100s, when Alexander I of Scotland ordered that the chapel should be dedicated and endowed. He died at Stirling Castle in 1124.

A strategically prized castle

Stirling Castle occupies an ideal defensive position sitting on top of a massive rocky outcrop with panoramic views of the surrounding countryside. The Highlands rise behind it, the Lowlands stretch in front of it and the River Forth runs beside it, flowing out to the Firth of Forth and the North Sea. The west face of the castle rock rises to 250 metres (820 ft), making it a formidable obstacle for any enemy. No wonder Stirling was such

▶ *The Gatehouse within the Forework has entries for pedestrians on either side of the main arched entrance.*

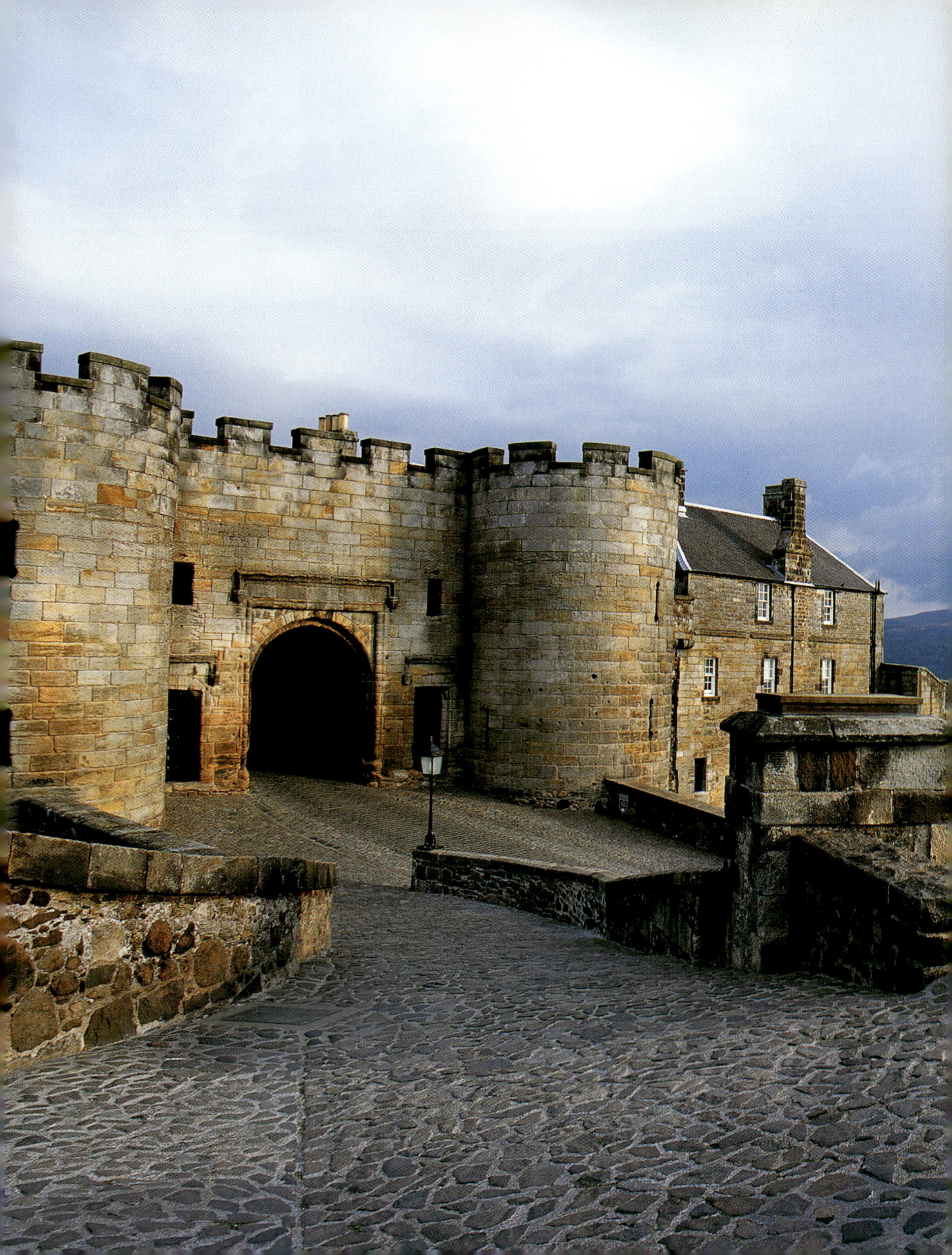

a prized possession to both the English and the Scots in the 13th and 14th centuries. Successive armies were prepared to fight for it since whichever country owned the castle also exercised a powerful control, physical and psychological, over most of Scotland.

The castle soon became a pawn in the hands of power-hungry monarchs. When the Scots king, William the Lyon, was captured on his way to England in 1174, Stirling was one of five Scottish castles demanded by the English as a ransom payment. The arrangement was revoked in 1189 and William died in the castle in 1214.

This was the start of a long phase in which the ownership of Stirling Castle switched between the English and Scots, usually to the accompaniment of much bloodshed. It was far too great a prize for Edward I of England to resist. In 1296 he seized it after the Scots king, John Balliol, was deposed.

Edward was a master of martial strategy and he appeared to take delight in humiliating the Scots in the hope of preventing more costly wars with them. However, he more than met his match in William Wallace, who led the Scots army in conjunction with Andrew Murray.

INTERESTING FEATURES

- *The Inner Close*
- *The bridge linking the Palace with the Great Hall*
- *The painted decoration in the Chapel Royal*
- *The King's Old Building*
- *The Great Hall*
- *The Great Kitchens*
- *The Palace*

Wallace and Murray knew the English troops would have to cross a timber bridge at Stirling, so they simply watched and waited from their vantage point on Abbey Craig. Their patience was rewarded when they mounted a successful ambush on 11 September 1297 and regained the castle. The Scots lost control of Stirling again the following year, but recaptured it in 1299. By 1303, Edward I had gained control of almost every important Scottish castle except Stirling, so he mounted an ambitious campaign to win it back, succeeding in July 1304.

Bannockburn

Edward I died in 1307 and the English throne passed to his son, Edward II, who was anything but a masterful leader. On the other hand, the Scots had lost William Wallace (who had the dubious honour of being the first person to be hanged, drawn

The Grand Battery, with its row of cannons, was built in the Outer Close in 1689.

and quartered by the English), but gained a magnificent leader in Robert the Bruce, who became King of Scotland in 1306. His brother, Edward, besieged Stirling Castle in 1314 and gave the English army a deadline: if they failed to relieve the castle by 24 June, the English had to surrender it to the Scots. This was an unthinkable proposition to Edward II and the opposing forces met on 23 and 24 June 1314 at the Battle of Bannockburn. The magnificent victory by the Scots at this battle is commemorated by a statue of Robert the Bruce on horseback on the site of the battle near Stirling Castle.

Ownership of the castle switched once more from the Scots to the English in the late 1330s, and was not regained by the Scots until 1342, under the leadership of Robert the Steward, later Robert II.

The palace is built

The building of the castle we see today began during the reign of James IV and

STIRLING CASTLE 169

included the Great Hall, the Forework and his personal residence, the King's Old Building.

James IV was one of the great builders of the Stewart line. He played a major role in the architectural history of Edinburgh Castle, Falkland Palace, the Palace of Holyroodhouse and Linlithgow Palace. He would undoubtedly have carried out more building work at Stirling had he not been killed at the Battle of Flodden Field on 9 September 1513. His infant son, James V, was crowned in the Chapel Royal at Stirling on 21 September 1513. The new King's first bride was Princess Madeleine, the daughter of Francis I of France, but she died soon after their wedding in 1537. James's second wife was Mary of Guise, whom he married in 1538 and brought home to Scotland. He built the palace within Stirling Castle for Mary. The palace is laid out around a central quadrangle, the 'Lion's Den'. The façades of the palace are heavily ornamented with statues and carvings of James V, as well as gods, the Devil, animals and mythical beasts.

Coronations and barracks

When James V died in December 1542, his baby daughter became Mary, Queen of Scots. She was crowned as a child at Stirling on 9 September 1543. It was the first time that the 'Honours of Scotland' – the crown, sceptre and sword of state – were all used at a coronation.

Mary was forced to abdicate from the Scottish throne on 24 July 1567 in favour of her baby son, James VI. He was crowned at the Church of the Holy Rude, the parish church of the burgh of Stirling, on 29 July 1567 and spent much of his childhood at the castle. When James VI became James I of England in 1603, he moved to England and returned to Scotland only once, in 1617. Scottish castles, including Stirling, fell into disrepair and were only renovated on the

◀ *Although the castle was a fortress, its gardens also offered recreation and relaxation to its inhabitants.*

170 SCOTLAND

▲ *Within the Inner Close, the King's Old Building stands at right angles to the Chapel Royal, which is to the right of the picture.*

rare occasion when a monarch was due to visit. Stirling's defences were strengthened between 1708 and 1714 to counter the Jacobite Risings, which aimed to put James Stuart, the Old Pretender, on the throne.

During the Napoleonic Wars at the turn of the 19th century, the Great Hall was converted into a barracks. The castle was later the base for the Argyll and Sutherland Highlanders until 1964. Today, much of Stirling Castle has been renovated and the building is an important example of medieval and Renaissance architecture.

information

Contact details

Stirling Castle
Castle Wynd
Stirling FK8 1EJ

+44 (0)1786 450 000

Stirling Castle
www.stirlingcastle.gov.uk

Transport links

Stirling

DUNFERMLINE ABBEY AND PALACE
Fife

Both Dunfermline Abbey and Dunfermline Palace have strong connections with the Scottish and English royal family. The abbey dates back to the 11th century and the palace to the 17th century. Although they are now little more than ruins, they are both steeped in history.

The abbey

Malcolm III and Queen Margaret were married at the church at Dunfermline c.1070. After the wedding, Margaret set up a religious community there and some Benedictine monks moved up from Canterbury in Kent. Margaret was later buried in the abbey in 1093.

The community remained fairly modest until David I, the son of Malcolm III and Margaret, granted it abbey status after 1128 as a tribute to his mother. The abbey became one of the richest in the country. The nave, built during this time and reminiscent of the Romanesque architecture of Durham Cathedral, still stands.

The abbey was ravaged by Edward I's troops in 1303 during the Wars of Independence. Rebuilding began almost immediately. Robert the Bruce supported work at the abbey and was later buried there in 1329. Work continued for over 250 years until the Reformation, when the abbey was sacked and fell into disrepair.

James VI of Scotland (later James I of England) took control of the abbey and its assets in 1593. He gave it to his wife, Anne. William Schaw was commissioned to

KEY DATES

✠ c.1070 Malcolm III and Margaret are married at Dunfermline Priory

✠ 1128 David I, their son, grants the building abbey status after this date

✠ 1303 Edward I's troops sack the abbey

✠ 1329 Robert the Bruce is buried there

✠ 1593 James VI of Scotland gives his wife, Anne, the abbey and work on a palace begins

✠ 1600 Charles I is born at the palace on 19 November; he is the last monarch to be born there

✠ 1633 The last repairs are made to the palace and abbey

▲ The abbey was built by David I to honour his mother, Margaret, who was later canonized.

rebuild the nave and construct a royal palace as Anne's main residence. Charles I, the last monarch to be born on Scottish soil, was born there in 1600. Sadly, after James VI came to the English throne, the palace was largely neglected, although it was repaired in 1633 just before a visit by Charles I. His son (the future Charles II) stayed there in 1650. Today the site is under the care of Historic Scotland.

INTERESTING FEATURES

- *The south range of the cloister*
- *The south wall of the palace*
- *The undercrofts below the kitchens*
- *The old gatehouse (housing the Historic Scotland Visitor Centre)*

information

Contact details

Dunfermline Palace and Abbey
18 St. Margaret St,
Dunfermline KY12 7PD

+44 (0)1383 739 026

Historic Scotland
www.historic-scotland.gov.uk/propertyresults/propertyoverview.htm?PropID=PL_108&PropName=Dunfermline%20Palace%20And%20Abbey

Transport links

Dunfermline

DUNFERMLINE ABBEY AND PALACE 173

SCONE PALACE
Perth

KEY DATES

✠ *1114 Augustinian priory founded by Alexander I*

✠ *1169 Priory becomes an abbey*

✠ *1296 Edward I of England's army steal the Stone of Destiny and take it to Westminster Abbey*

✠ *1488 James IV crowned at Scone Abbey on 26 June*

✠ *1559 Scone Abbey burned down by a Protestant mob*

✠ *1651 Charles II crowned King of Scotland on 1 January*

✠ *1803 William Atkinson starts to rebuild Scone as a Gothic palace*

✠ *1939 Scone is turned into a school*

✠ *1959 The Mansfield family return to live at Scone*

✠ *1966 Scone Palace opened to the public*

After the Romans left Scotland, the area around Scone in Perthshire became a major Pictish stronghold. The Picts, or 'painted people', were subdued by Kenneth MacAlpin, who was half Pictish himself and became King of the Picts in 843 and King of Scotland a couple of years later. There are suggestions that he brought the Stone of Destiny to Scone and set it on Moot Hill, where it became the crowning seat for coronations. The first recorded instance of a Scottish coronation was that of King Lulach in August 1057, who was crowned while seated on the Stone of Destiny at Scone. In 1114, Alexander I founded an Augustinian priory at Scone, which became an abbey in 1169. This was the home of the Stone of Destiny when not in use as a coronation stone.

Edward I of England was infuriated by the rebellion in 1296 of John Balliol, the man he had appointed as the Scottish king (thus turning him into a lapdog) and who now sided with the French against him. Edward's murderous army marched into Scotland and brought the country to its knees. Seizing the Stone of Destiny, Edward took it to Westminster Abbey, an act that symbolized what he saw as Scotland's subjugation by England. The stone stayed at Westminster Abbey until it was returned to Scotland and placed with due ceremony in Edinburgh Castle in 1996.

Changes in ownership

Despite the absence of the Stone of Destiny, Scottish monarchs continued to be crowned at Scone Abbey until Edinburgh became an important power base in the 15th century. The last purely Scottish king to be crowned at Scone was James IV in 1488. The exiled Charles II was crowned King of Scotland at Scone in 1651, although the original abbey had burned down in 1559 and been replaced by Scone Palace. In 1600, the land was given to Sir David Murray, an ancestor of the Earls of Mansfield who live there today.

▲ Scottish parliaments met at Scone Abbey, where the palace now stands, between 1210 and 1452.

INTERESTING FEATURES

✠ Replica Stone of Destiny on Moot Hill
✠ The Chapel
✠ The hangings in the Lennox Room
✠ The Long Gallery
✠ The porcelain collection in the Library

ⓘ information

Contact details

Scone Palace
Perth
PH2 6BD

☎ +44 (0)1738 552300

Scone Palace
www.scone-palace.co.uk

Transport links

🚆 5 km (3 miles) from Perth

✈ Scone Palace is a 40-minute drive from Edinburgh International Airport

🚗 From Dundee, Edinburgh or Glasgow, follow the signs for the 'A93 Braemar'. Scone is 3 km (2 miles) north of Perth

🚌 Stagecoach 3 and 58 from Perth

SCONE PALACE

GLAMIS CASTLE
Angus

KEY DATES

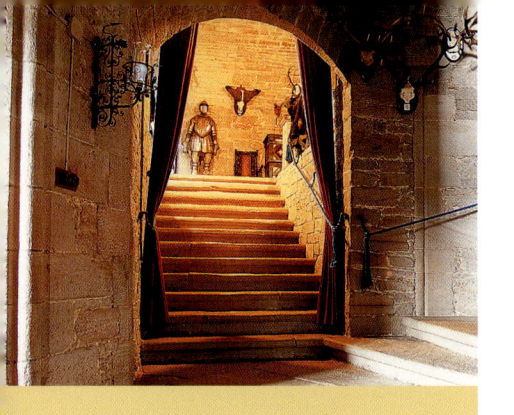

- 1034 Malcolm II dies at the castle on 25 November
- 1372 Robert II gives land to Sir John Lyon
- 1400 East Wing is built
- 1440 The Tower is built
- 1537–42 Castle confiscated by James V
- 1562 Visit by Mary, Queen of Scots
- c.1600 The castle is remodelled and enlarged
- 1688 Family Chapel completed
- 1716 Visit by the Old Pretender in February
- 1900 Hon. Elizabeth Angela Marguerite Bowes-Lyon (later Queen Elizabeth The Queen Mother) is born on 4 August
- 1923 The Duke and Duchess of York spend their honeymoon at Glamis
- 1930 Princess Margaret Rose born at the castle on 21 August

The exterior of Glamis Castle, with its turrets, parapets and backdrop of the Grampian Mountains, is rich in atmosphere and magic. This is a castle steeped in Scottish history and redolent with legend. The interior of the castle, snug within its thick walls, is even more atmospheric. It is therefore highly appropriate that Glamis is alleged to be the most haunted stately home in Britain.

Another persistent rumour is that a member of the Bowes-Lyon family, which has owned Glamis for 600 years, was once walled up alive in a secret chamber, believed to be somewhere near the crypt (legend has it that there are more windows on the outside of the castle than can be found inside, hence the theory of secret rooms). It is hardly surprising that Shakespeare set Duncan's murder at the hands of Macbeth at Glamis, even though this is historically incorrect.

The home of kings

Glamis Castle was originally a hunting lodge for Scottish kings. Malcolm II died there in 1034 after being fatally wounded in a battle. King Robert II gave the land to Sir John Lyon in 1372 in gratitude for services rendered; four years later, Sir John married Joanna, Robert's daughter, and was given a barony. His son, who was also called Sir John, began building what is the East Wing of the present castle in about 1400. The Tower was added

▶ *The castle was remodelled in the early 1600s and the Drawing Room dates from this period. The ceiling was made by local craftsmen in 1621.*

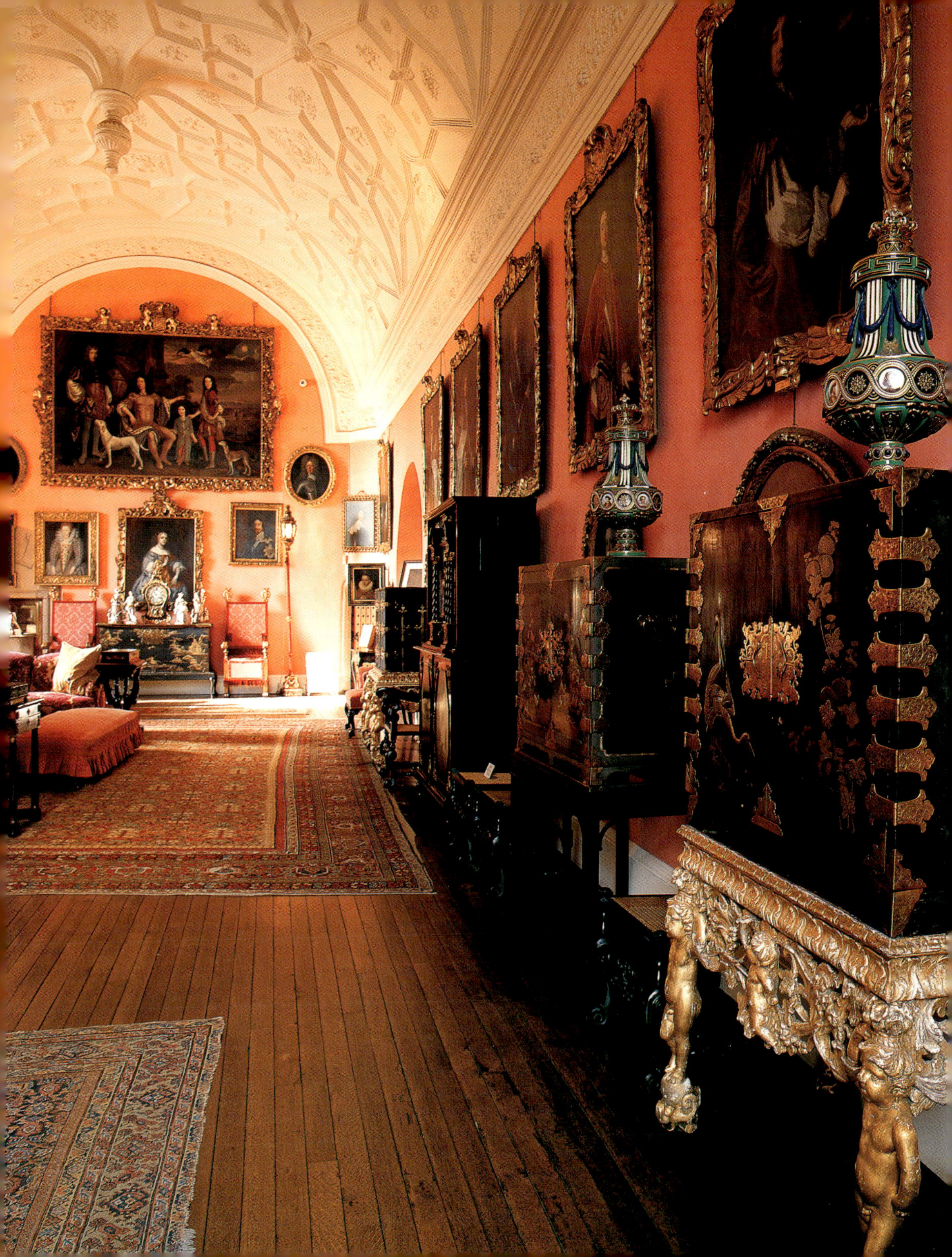

◀ *Duncan's Hall is so-named because it was once thought to be the site of his murder by Macbeth, who was immortalized in Shakepeare's play.*

witchcraft and she was eventually burned at the stake outside Edinburgh Castle. Her young son was also locked up under sentence of death, and James confiscated Glamis Castle and lived there himself between 1537 and 1542. After James died on 14 December 1542, Parliament released the young 7th Lord Glamis and restored the castle to him, but by then many of its treasures were missing.

The Old Pretender

Glamis had a chequered history during the 16th and 17th centuries, thanks to the financial whims of its successive owners. By the time Glamis was restored to solvency in the late 1600s, its owners were styled the Earls of Strathmore and Kinghorne, and have been known as such ever since.

One of the most colourful royal visitors to the castle was the Old Pretender, James Francis Edward Stuart, who stayed there in February 1716. The exiled son of James II of England and VII of Scotland, he protested throughout his life that he was the rightful heir to the British throne, even to the point of being proclaimed James III of England and VIII of Scotland while in France in

in 1440 and the castle was greatly extended in 1600, with further additions made later in the 17th century in a style now called Scottish Baronial.

Throughout its life, Glamis Castle has had strong links with Scottish history. One of its most sombre connections took place during the reign of James V. He was a man with a chip on his shoulder and the power to exact his revenge on whoever he felt deserved it. One focus of his bitterness was the Douglas family, into which his mother, Margaret Tudor, married after the death of her first husband, James IV, at the Battle of Flodden in 1513. The young James V had a wretched childhood and never allowed himself, or anyone else, to forget it. James wrongly imprisoned Lady Janet Douglas, the widow of the 6th Lord Glamis, for

▶ *The crypt was originally the lower hall, in which the castle servants ate and slept.*

178 SCOTLAND

1701. During his visit to Glamis, he participated in the ancient custom of 'touching for the king's evil' in the Chapel. It was commonly believed that a true king or queen could successfully cure someone who was suffering from scrofula, or the 'king's evil', simply by touching them. Much to the delight of his Jacobite supporters (and, presumably, the sufferers themselves), the Old Pretender duly proved his claim to the throne.

INTERESTING FEATURES

- ✠ *The crypt*
- ✠ *The Drawing Room*
- ✠ *The Chapel*
- ✠ *The Queen Mother's Apartments*
- ✠ *Duncan's Hall*

GLAMIS CASTLE

The Queen Mother

During the 20th century, Glamis became famous as the ancestral home of Lady Elizabeth Bowes-Lyon, who was to marry Prince Albert, Duke of York, in 1923. Following the abdication of his brother, Edward VIII, in 1936, Prince Albert succeeded to the throne as George VI and Elizabeth became the first Queen Consort to have been born in Britain since Henry VIII's reign. In 1952, after George VI's death, she became HM Queen Elizabeth The Queen Mother, a title she held until her death on 30 March 2002.

Elizabeth was born in 1900 into an aristocratic golden age obliterated by the First World War. Her 14th birthday coincided with the outbreak of war, during which Glamis was converted into a military hospital. Elizabeth helped to look after the many wounded soldiers who stayed there. In 1915, her brother, Fergus, was killed at the Battle of Loos, and later another brother, Michael, was taken prisoner of war. For the rest of Elizabeth's life, as with so many of her generation, the First World War held special significance for her.

◀ Many legends are connected with Glamis Castle because it has a potent atmosphere of mystery and magic.

admirers; the most notable, the Duke of York. Bertie, as his family knew him, was a shy, stammering young man plagued by nervous indigestion and dominated by his father, George V. However, the sweet-natured young duke had remarkable patience and persistence, as he had to wait two years for Elizabeth to accept his marriage proposal.

The Duke and Duchess of York, as they were known until 1936 when they became King George VI and Queen Elizabeth, regularly used the suite of three rooms at Glamis today known as the Queen Mother's Apartments. They spent the latter half of their honeymoon at Glamis and their younger daughter, Princess Margaret, was born there in 1930 – the first royal baby born in Scotland since 1600, when Charles I was born at Dunfermline Palace.

The Queen Mother always kept up her ties to her old family home. An exhibition has been set up at Glamis in her memory.

Pretty, amusing, charming and vivacious, the young Lady Elizabeth Bowes-Lyon was the most popular debutante in post-war London. She had a string of devoted

information

Contact details

Glamis Castle
Glamis, by Forar
Angus DD8 1RJ

+44 (0)1307 840393

Glamis Castle
www.glamis-castle.co.uk

Transport links

19 km (12 miles) from Dundee

19 km (12 miles) from Dundee via the A90/A94

GLAMIS CASTLE **181**

FALKLAND PALACE
Falkland

KEY DATES

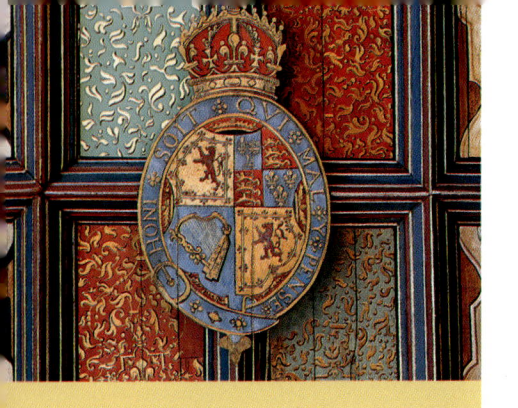

- ✠ *12th century* Castle built on the site
- ✠ *1402* Death of Prince David in the first palace in March
- ✠ *1501–41* The second Falkland Palace built
- ✠ *1539* Royal tennis court built
- ✠ *1541* Mary of Guise gives birth to her second son in the palace in April
- ✠ *1542* Death of James V at Falkland Palace on 14 December
- ✠ *1654* Destruction of the east range of the palace
- ✠ *1887* Restoration work carried out on the palace by the 3rd Marquis of Bute
- ✠ *1947–52* Garden designed and planted by Percy Crane
- ✠ *1952* The National Trust for Scotland acquires the palace
- ✠ *1970* Falkland is made Scotland's first conservation area

Built in 16th-century French Renaissance style, Falkland Palace was a favourite haunt of Scottish monarchs. James I of Scotland had seized the castle from its owners in 1425. His son, James II, gave the earldom of Fife to his queen, Mary of Gueldres, and Falkland Palace became a favourite residence of the Scottish court. Mary made various improvements to the palace after the death of James II in 1460, including what may have been the first gallery to be built in Scotland.

Building a new palace

Work started on a new palace in 1501 under the direction of James IV of Scotland, until he died in 1513. The half-finished palace languished, neglected, for several years until James V married Mary of Guise in 1538 and more work was rapidly carried out. Much of the existing building was remodelled and new rooms added. Each mason had a slightly different architectural style, creating some

INTERESTING FEATURES

- ✠ The Gatehouse and Keeper's Apartments
- ✠ The Chapel Royal
- ✠ The King's Bedchamber
- ✠ The Queen's Room

▶ *Falkland Palace was a tranquil retreat from the bustle and smells of Edinburgh for the Scottish nobility.*

interesting contrasts. The turreted Gatehouse, for instance, has a different appearance to the medallions and other carvings on the north front of the courtyard.

Unlucky connections

Work on the palace was completed by 1541, and in April, Mary of Guise gave birth to her second son in the palace. The child died eight days later, and his older brother, James, also died that April. James V was left without a direct heir until Mary gave birth to a daughter, also named Mary, on 8 December 1542 at Linlithgow Palace. Once again tragedy accompanied the birth: James V died six days later at Falkland Palace. Despite this, both Mary of Guise and her daughter, Mary, Queen of Scots, had many happy times at the palace. They both considered it to be a place of refuge and relaxation. The oldest royal tennis court still in use can be found there. It was created in 1539 for James V.

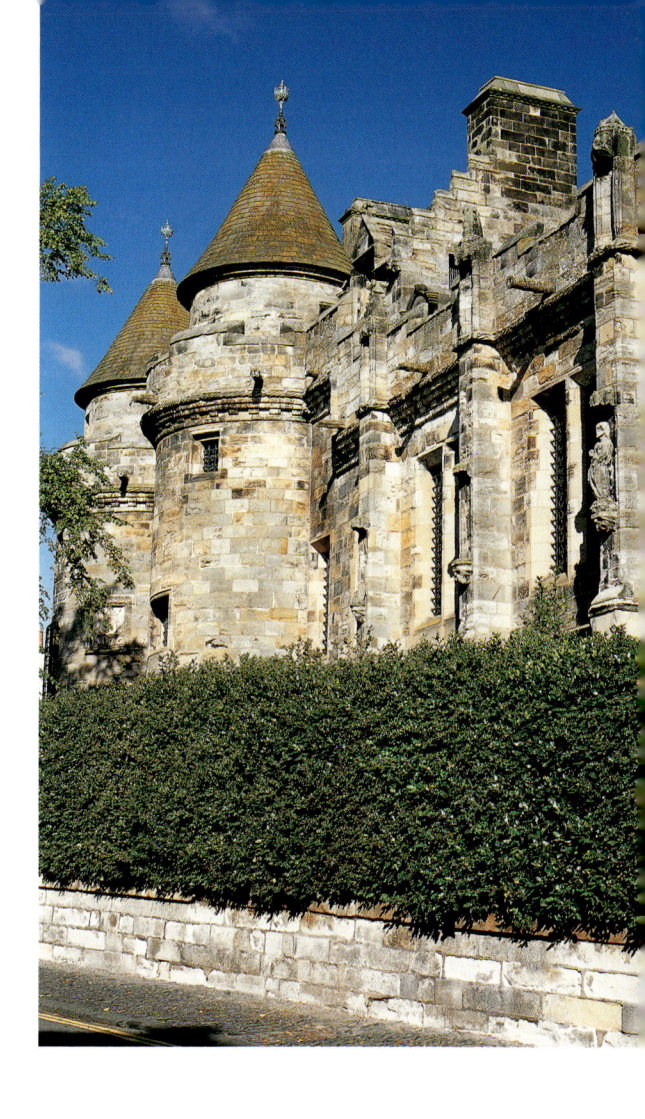

ⓘ information

Contact details

Falkland Palace
Cupar
KY15 7BU

☎ +44 (0)844 4932186

National Trust for Scotland
www.nts.org.uk/Property/93

Transport links

Ladybank Railway Station

From the rail station take 66/67 Stagecoach Fife bus service to Cupar. Stops 100 metres (109 yards) from Palace Other Stagecoach buses: 35, 36, 36B, 66/67

BALMORAL CASTLE
Aberdeenshire

KEY DATES

✠ 1840 Marriage of Queen Victoria to Prince Albert of Saxe-Coburg and Gotha on 10 February

✠ 1852 Prince Albert buys Balmoral for Queen Victoria

✠ 1853 The foundation stone of the new castle is laid by Queen Victoria on 28 September

✠ 1856 The new castle is completed

✠ 1861 Death of Prince Albert on 14 December

✠ 1878 Ballochbuie Forest bought by Queen Victoria and added to the Balmoral Estate

✠ 1883 Death of John Brown on 27 March

✠ 1901 Death of Queen Victoria on 22 January

✠ 1974 Area around Loch Muick and Lochnagar is designated as a wildlife reserve, managed by the Scottish Wildlife Trust

Scotland, declared Prince Albert, was 'very German-looking'. Its wooded hills and valleys reminded him of his native Bavaria and the thought of establishing a private residence there greatly appealed to him and his wife, Queen Victoria. The royal couple fell in love with the Scottish Highlands during their visits there in the 1840s, not long after they were married, and, although it was a long way from London, the journey had been made much easier by the recent advent of the railway. They were particularly interested in the area around the River Dee, known today as Royal Deeside, partly because it had the lowest rainfall in Scotland.

Life at Balmoral

The acquisition of the estate at Balmoral was not an easy one, with negotiations lasting several years before the sale was finally completed in 1852. There was already a 15th-century castle on the site, but it was deemed too small and work began almost immediately on a much grander replacement. White granite, from the nearby quarries at Glen Gelder, was used and the present building was erected under the precise and painstaking direction of Prince Albert, who even went so far as to design a Balmoral tartan. Queen Victoria loved Balmoral, declaring that 'all seemed to breathe freedom and peace'. Both were important to her, as she

▶ *Balmoral Castle is part of the Balmoral Estate, a working estate that covers about 20,000 hectares (50,000 acres) and is privately owned and funded by the Queen.*

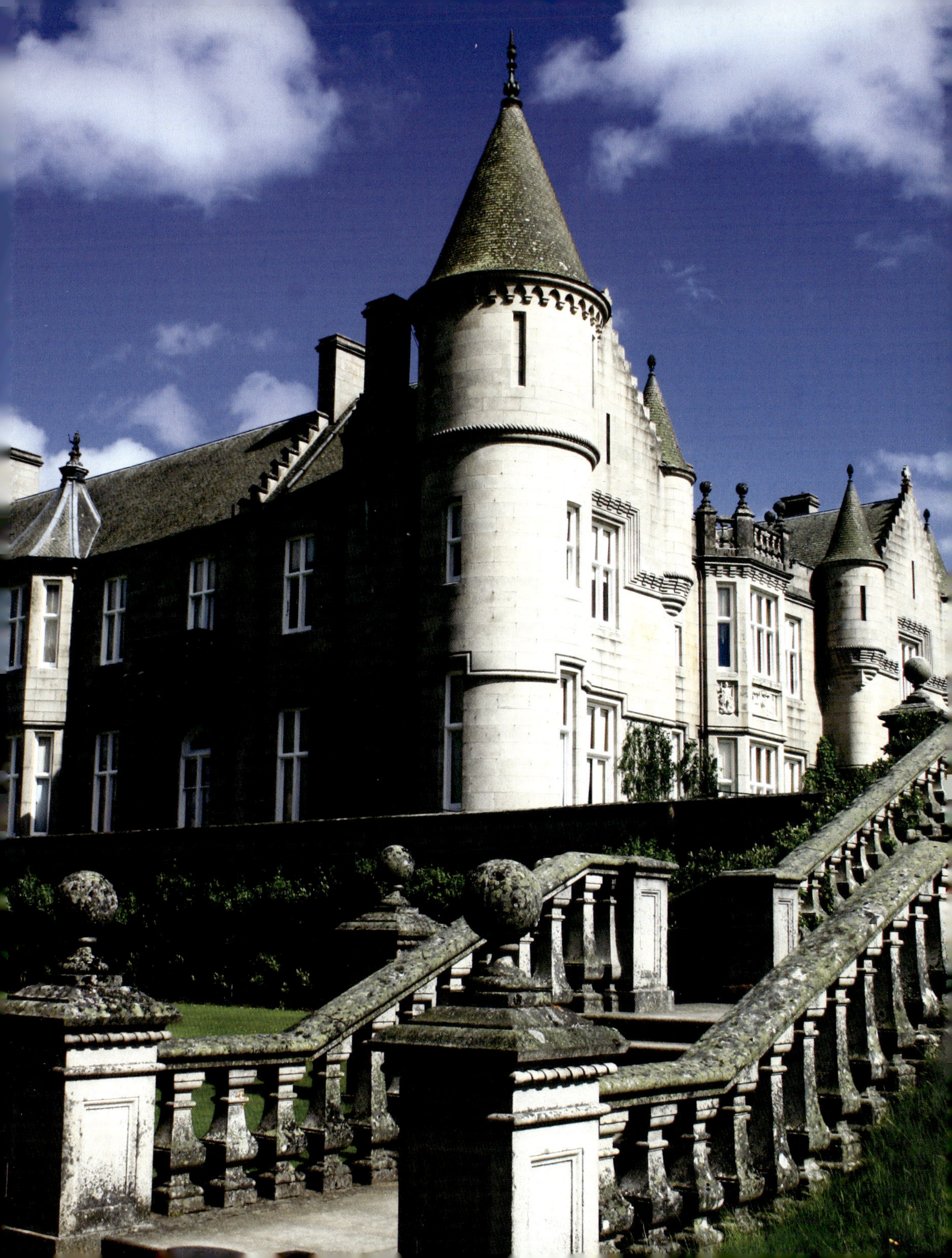

was aware of the need for a private home in which she and Albert could enjoy a simple life with their family, away from the formality of Buckingham Palace. They were also anxious to set an example of Christian family life to the nation, showing they were willing to work hard for the privileges of their position.

Grief and friendship

Prince Albert died in 1861 and left Balmoral to Victoria. She began to fill the grounds with a series of memorials. There were cairns (pyramids of stones) to commemorate Albert's death and other, happier events, plus statues and seats, but not all the memorials were for Albert. One statue was erected in the memory of John Brown, Queen Victoria's faithful Scottish gillie and a cause of gossip in her later years.

Four years after the death of Albert, Victoria appointed Brown as her 'permanent personal attendant', and moved him south from Balmoral to Windsor, London and Osborne. At the time it caused great scandal and there were arch references in high society to Queen Victoria as 'Mrs Brown'.

Balmoral is principally a private home in which the royal family can relax away from the public and the world media.

Whatever the precise nature of their relationship, there is no denying that they enjoyed an easy familiarity. His alcoholism, combined with Victoria's favouritism, made him extremely unpopular with the rest of the court, although he seemed not to care about such things. Despite his gruff manner, Victoria doted on him. John Brown died at Windsor on 27 March 1883 from complications caused by his chronic alcoholism, and his death plunged Victoria into deep mourning once again.

Among the many cherished mementoes that were laid in Victoria's coffin in 1901, were a photograph of Brown and a lock of his hair. Following Victoria's instructions, both of these were placed in her left hand and discreetly hidden by flowers from Queen Alexandra.

Balmoral today

Successive generations of royalty have continued to improve and change the castle and its grounds, making their own mark on its history. After becoming king, one of Edward VII's first actions was to have the statue of John Brown moved to a far-off corner of the estate, well out of view. His daughter-in-law, Queen Mary, oversaw the creation of a flower garden and, much more recently, the Duke of Edinburgh created a water garden and enlarged the flower and vegetable gardens.

Balmoral is still used by the royal family for private holidays each August and September, although heads of state occasionally visit the Queen there.

> ### INTERESTING FEATURES
>
> ✠ *Plaque on the front lawn showing the position of the previous castle*
> ✠ *The Ballroom exhibition*
> ✠ *The Carriage Hall exhibition*
> ✠ *The grounds and gardens*

information

Contact details

Balmoral Castle
Ballater
Aberdeenshire
AB35 5TB

+44 (0)13397 42534

Balmoral Castle
www.balmoralcastle.com

Transport links

Aberdeen, 80 km (50 miles)

From Aberdeen travel on the A93 towards Braemar to Crathie. On left is the Tourist Information Centre

THE CASTLE OF MEY
Caithness

A relatively recent royal residence, the Castle of Mey was acquired by the newly widowed Her Majesty Queen Elizabeth The Queen Mother in 1952. At that time it was in a poor condition and still known as Barrogill Castle. The Queen Mother spent time there every August and October for most of the next 50 years. She carefully renovated it and established its impressive gardens and parklands. She also changed it back to its original name.

A strategically prized castle

The castle was built on a Z-plan between 1566 and 1572 by George, 4th Earl of Caithness, for his son, William Sinclair. William was murdered by his brother, John, while visiting the family seat, Girnigoe Castle, in 1573. When John was himself murdered, the castle passed to George Sinclair, his younger brother, who changed its name to Barrogill.

For the next 100 years, Barrogill was the main seat of the Earls of Caithness. The 12th Earl commissioned William Burn to renovate and add to the existing castle and during that time the dining room and grand entrance to the castle were constructed. George, the 15th Earl, who died without heirs, left the castle to his friend, F. G. Heathcote, in 1889. In 1928, the castle was bought by Captain Imbert-Terry and was used as an officers' rest home during the Second World War. Queen Elizabeth The Queen Mother bought the house

KEY DATES

- 1566 Work begins on the castle, the home of William Sinclair
- 1573 William is murdered and the castle passes to his brother, John, then to his brother, George, who renames it Barrogill Castle
- 1889 The castle passes out of the family of the Earls of Caithness
- 1928 Captain Imbert-Terry buys the castle
- 1952 Queen Elizabeth The Queen Mother buys the castle
- 1966 The Castle of Mey Trust is set up
- 2002 The castle is opened to the public

▲ The Castle of Mey was bought by the Queen Mother in 1952, following the death of her husband, King George VI.

in 1952 and over the next three years renovated and restored the building (which comprises some 38 rooms, including 15 bedrooms) and surrounding land. In 1958 she added to the estate when she purchased Longoe Farm.

Today the castle is administered by the Castle of Mey Trust, established in 1996. It was opened to the public in 2002.

INTERESTING FEATURES

- The corbelled turrets
- The walled gardens
- The parklands
- The round arched entrance to the courtyard

information

Contact details

The Castle of Mey
Thurso
Caithness
Scotland
KW14 8XH

+44 (0)1847 851473

The Castle of Mey
www.castleofmey.org.uk

Transport links

On the A836 in Canisbay, about 24 km (15 miles) east of Thurso and 9.5 km (6 miles) west of John O'Groats

THE CASTLE OF MEY 189

INDEX

Page numbers in **bold** are main references. Page numbers in *italic* refer to illustrations.

Adelaide, Queen 51, 99
Albert, Prince 12, 27, 52, 54, 56-7, 68, 69, 184, 186
Alexandra, Princess 99
Alexandra, Queen 10, 13, 23, 187
Anne, Princess Royal 96, 99
Anne, Queen 24, 33–4, 86, 88-91, 98, 122–4
Anne of Cleves 43
Anne of Denmark 82, 83–4, 118, 172–3
Argyll and Sutherland Highlanders 171
Arlington House 66
Arthur's Seat 146, 152
Astor, William Waldorf 40, 43
Atkinson, William 174
'auld alliance' 155

Baillie, Lady 44, 45
Ballochbuie Forest 184
Balmoral Castle **184–7**, *185*, *186*
Bannockburn, Battle of 166, 169
Banqueting House 98, **114–17**, *115*, *117*
Barrogill Castle 188
Barry, Charles 102, 109
Beatrice, Princess (daughter of Queen Victoria) 61
Beaumaris Castle **138–9**, *139*
Bella Court 118
Berkeley Castle **126–7**, *127*
Besant, C.H. 70
Blenheim, Battle of 122
Blenheim Palace **122–5**, *123*, *125*
Blood, Colonel Thomas 72, 81
Blore, Edward 68, 69
Blücher, Marshal 99
Boleyn, Anne 30, 40–3, 78, 79, 106
Bonnie Prince Charlie *see* Stuart, Charles
Bothwell, James, 4th Earl of 152, 158, 159
Bowes-Lyon family 176
British parliamentary system 109
Brown, John 184, 186–7
Brown, Lancelot Capability 34, 122
Buckingham House 64, 66, 67
Buckingham Palace 26, 51, 62, **64–71**, *65*, *66*, *69*, *85*, *91*, *99*

Bullen, George 40, 43
Bullen family 40
Burghley, William Cecil, Lord 16
Burn, William 188

Caernarfon Castle **132–7**, *133*, *134*, *136*
Carisbrooke Castle **58–61**, *59*, *60*
Carlton House, London 48, 50, 66–7
Caroline, Queen 34, 36, 46, 49, 91
Castellated Palace 38
Castle Howard 122
Castle of Maidens 146
Catherine of Aragon 30, 42, 44
Catherine of Braganza 82, 85
Chambers, Sir William 24, 38, 84
Charles I 23, 31, 58, 84, 98, 106, 112, 114, 116, 150–1, 162, 165, 172, 173
Charles II 20, 23–4, 33, 75, 77, 80, 81, 85, 116, 151, 159, 160, 173, 174, 175
Charles, Prince of Wales 15, 71, 101, 132, 137
Charlotte, Queen 24, 36, 38, 39
Chaucer, Geoffrey 109, 112
Churchill, Winston 71, 106, 122, 124–5
Civil War 31, 85, 119, 126, 127, 131, 132, 136, 138, 139, 159
Clarence House 96, 99, 100–1
Clay, Charles 94
Conwy Castle 135
Court of St James 96
Courtauld family 110, 112–13
Cowper, Hon Charles Spencer 10
Crane, Percy 182
Cromwell, Oliver 28, 33, 82, 85, 151, 167
crown jewels 80-1
Cruikshank, George 46
Cubitt, Thomas 52, 54, 68
Culloden, Battle of 161
Cumberland, Duke of 48

Darnley, Henry Stuart, Lord 142, 156, 158–9
David I 148, 152, 172
David II 149
Denmark House 82, 83-5
Diana, Princess of Wales (formerly Spencer) 10, 15, 71, 86
Domesday Book 44, 110
Douglas family 178
Duncan, King 176

Dunfermline Abbey and Palace **172–3**, *173*
Dyce, William: frescoes *107*

Edinburgh: Royal Mile 146, 150, 152
Edinburgh Castle *141*, **146–51**, *147*, *149*, *150*, *151*, *152*, *170*
  Crown Square 149-50
  St Margaret's Chapel 146, *146*, 148
Edward the Confessor 102
Edward I 44, 60, 79, 120, 128, 132–6, 138, 146, 148, 162, 166, 168, 169, 172, 174
Edward II (1st Prince of Wales) 44, 106, 110, 126–7, 132, 135, 169
Edward III 20-2
Edward IV 22, 23, 76, 77, 112
Edward V 72, 77, 79
Edward VI 31, 45, 79, 82
Edward VII (formerly Prince of Wales) 10, 12–13, 14, 23, 57, 64, 70, 106, 137, 187
Edward VIII (later Duke of Windsor) 13, 14, 70, 137, 180
Edward, Duke of Kent 91-2
Edward, Prince (son of Elizabeth II) 23
Eleanor of Castile 44, 135
Elizabeth I 16, *18*, 19, 31, 35, 42, 60-1, 76, 78–9, 82, 83, 98, 112, 114, 118, 150, 156, 159
Elizabeth II 15, 36, 39, 64, 71, 100-1
Elizabeth, Queen Mother 96, 101, 106, 176, 180–1, 188, 189
Eltham Lodge 112
Eltham Palace 62, **110–13**, *111*, *113*
Ethelbert IV 44
Evelyn, John 112

Falkland Palace 164, 170, **182–3**, *183*
Fawkes, Guy 106, 109
Fitzharding, Robert 126
Fitzherbert, Maria 46, 48-9
FitzOsbern family 58
Flodden Field, Battle of 164
Fortrey, Samuel 36
Francis II of France 156
Frederick II 75
Frederick, Prince of Wales 33, 38
Frogmore 20, 24, 27
Gentileschi, Orazio 119
George I 24, 34, 86, 88–91, 92, 93–4, 98-9

190 ROYAL BRITAIN

George II 24, 34, 36, 38, 66, 86, 91, 100
George III 23, 24–6, 34, 36, 38, 39, 48, 66, 67, 91, 96
George IV (formerly Prince Regent) 23, 26, 46, 48, 50–1, 64, 66–8, 71, 91, 99, 161
George V 10, 13-14, 95, 137, 152, 181
George VI 10, 14-15, 70–1, 101, 180-1
Gibbons, Grinling 24
Gilray, James 46
Girnigoe Castle 188
Glamis Castle **176–81**, *177, 178, 179, 180-1*
Glorious Revolution 144
Glyn Dwr, Owain 131, 132, 138
Goring House 64
Great Fire of London 33
Greenwich Palace 31, 112
Grey, Lady Jane 79

Hampton Court Palace **28–35**, *29, 32,* 88, 95
Handel, George Frideric 100
Harlech Castle 120, *121,* **128–31**, *129, 130,* 135
Harold, King 105
Harry, Prince 101
Hastings, Battle of 105
Hatfield House 19
Hatfield Palace **16–19**, *17*
Hawksmoor, Nicholas 88, 99, 124
Henrietta Maria, Queen 31, 82, 84, 85, 118-19
Henry I 20, 58, 60
Henry II 20, 126
Henry II of France 156
Henry III 75, 79, 128, 132
Henry IV 110, 112
Henry V 131
Henry VI 22-3, 72, 76, 118, 162
Henry VII 23
Henry VIII 16, 23, 28, 30-1, 34, 40, 43, 44, 78, 96, 100, 102, 106, 109, 112, 114, 136, 154
Hess, Rudolf 72
Hever Castle **40-3**, *41, 42*
Holland, Henry 46-8, 49
Holyrood Abbey 152
Holyroodhouse 146, 150, **152-61**, *153, 154, 157, 158, 160,* 170
Honours of Scotland 146, 170
House of Commons 102
House of Lords 102, *104*
Houses of Parliament 102
Howard, Catherine 79

Howard, Elizabeth 40
Humphrey, Duke of Gloucester 118

Impert-Terry, Captain 188
Isabella, Queen 110, 126

Jacobite Risings 151, 171
Jacobites 144
James I of Scotland 162, 182
James I (VI of Scotland) 16, 31, 74-5, 78, 83, 116, 118, 146, 150, 158, 159, 164, 170, 172
James II 86, 98, 144, 160, 162, 182
James III of Scotland 142, 149, 162, 164
James IV of Scotland 154-5, 162,164, 166, 169-70, 174, 175, 178, 182
James V of Scotland 152, 154-5, 162, 164, 166, 170, 176, 178, 182, 183
James of St George, Master 128, 134, 138
Janyns, Henry 22
Jersey, Lady 49
Joan of Navarre 110, 112
John, King 128
John Balliol, King of Scotland 168
John of Padua 83
Jones, Inigo 82, 84, 114, 116, 118
Jonson, Ben 84, 109

Kenneth MacAlpin, King of Scotland 174
Kensington Palace **86-95**, *87, 89, 90, 93, 94*
Kent, William 34, 38, 86, 92, 93-4, 95
Keppel, Arnold Joost van 95
Kew House (White House) 38
Kew Palace **36-9**, *37, 39*
Kircaldy of Grange, Sir William 150
Knights Hospitallers of St John of Jerusalem 28
Knox, John 156

Lambeth Palace 68
Lancaster House 99
Law Courts 102
Ledian 44
Leeds Castle **44-5**, *45*
Levett, Sir Richard 36
Linlithgow Palace **162-5**, *163, 165,* 170
Llewelyn ap Iowerth (the Great) 128
Llywelyn ap Gruffydd (the Last) 128, 132
London:
 Roman wall 72
 Strand and riverside 83
London Zoo 76
Louis IX 75

Lulach, King 174
Lyon, Sir John 176

Macbeth 176
Madeleine Valois 155, 170
Magna Carta 126
Maitland, James, 1st Duke of Lauderdale 159
Malcolm II 176
Malcolm III 146, 172
Mansfield family 174, 175
Marble Arch 64, 68
Margaret, Princess 71, 86, 176, 181
Margaret, St, Queen of Scotland 146-8, 152, 172
Margaret of Anjou 118
Margaret of Denmark 162
Margaret Tudor 154, 156, 178
Marlborough, John Churchill, 1st Duke of 122, 124
Marlborough, Sarah, Duchess of 122-4
Marlborough House, London 12
Mary I 78-9, 96, 118
Mary II 28, 33, 35, 86, 88, 95, 117, 144
Mary, Queen (consort of George V) 12, 13, 51, 70, 95, 152, 187
Mary, Queen of Scots 140, 142, 150, 152, 155-9, 161, 164, 170, 176, 183
Mary of Guise 155, 162, 170, 182, 183
menagerie 75-6
Mey, the Castle of **188-9**, *189*
More, Sir Thomas 106
Mortimer, Roger 110, 126
Murray, Andrew 168-9

Nash, John 48, 50, 64, 67-8, 70, 96, 99
National Maritime Museum 118, 119
Nicholson, Harold 13
Normans 72, 105
Nottingham House 86, 88

Odo, Bishop of Bayeux 58, 110
Old Pretender see Stuart, James
Order of the Garter 22
Osborne House **52-7**, *53, 55, 56,* 69

Palladio, Andrea 118
Parr, Catherine 31
Philip IV of France 110
Philip, Prince, Duke of Edinburgh 187
Philip of Savoy 134
Picts 174
Placentia 118
Princes in the Tower 72, 77
Pugin, Augustus 102, 109
Pyke, John 94

INDEX **191**

Queen Victoria Memorial 70
Queen's House, Greenwich 62, **118-19**, *119*

Raleigh, Sir Walter 109
Rhys-Jones, Sophie 23
Rich, Colonel Nathaniel 112
Richard II 106, 112
Richard III 77
Richmond Lodge 38
Richmond Palace 98
Rizzio, David 152, 156, 157-8
Robert the Bruce 149, 169, 172
Robert de Crevecoeur 44
Robert II of Scotland 169, 176
Robert of Rhuddlan 132, 135
Royal, Princess see Anne, Princess
Royal Council 109
Royal Mint 72
Royal Naval Asylum 118, 119
Royal Osborne see Osborne House
Royal Pavilion, Brighton 9, **46-51**, *47, 49, 50, 52*, 68
Rubens, Peter Paul 114, 116, 119

St Georges d'Esperanche 134
St James's Hospital 96
St James's Palace 24, 26, 62, 66, 83, **96-101**, *97, 98, 100-1*
St James's Park 96, 98
Salisbury, 3rd Marquis (and 9th Earl) 19
Salisbury, Robert Cecil, Earl of 16, 19
Salisbury Crags 152
Sandringham House 8, **10-15**, *11, 13, 14*
Schaw, William 172-3
Scone Palace **174-5**, *175*
Scott, Sir Walter 146
Seymour, Edward 82-3
Seymour, Jane 23, 31
Shakespeare, William 126

Shaw, Sir John 112
Sinclair, William 188
Singh, Bai Ram 57
Somerset House **82-5**, *84*
Spencer, Lady Diana see Diana, Princess of Wales
Stafford House 99
Stirling Bridge, Battle of 166, 169
Stirling Castle **164**, *166-71*, *167*, *168*, *170*, *171*
Stone, Nicholas 84
Stone of Destiny 146, 174-5
Stuart, Charles Edward (Bonnie Prince Charlie) 140, 142, 144, 151, 152, 160-1, 162
Stuart, James Francis Edward (Old Pretender) 144, 151, 171, 176, 178-9
Stuarts 142-4

Thackeray, William 46
Thames, River 86-8
Theobalds House 16
Thynne, John 83
Tower of London 63, **72-81**, *73, 74, 75, 76*
  Chapel Royal of St John the Evangelist 74
  Chapel Royal of St Peter ad Vincula 79, 80
  Queen's House 78
Traquair House **142-5**, *143, 145*
Trevisa, John 126

Van Groeningen, Isabelle 110
Vanbrugh, Sir John 85, 88, 99, 122, 124
VE Day 71
Victoria, Queen 10, 12, 27, 36, 51, 52, 54-7, 68, 69, 70, 86, 92, 95, 152, 161, 166, 184-7
Victoria Tower Gardens, London *108*

Wales: princes of 132, 135
Wallace, William 166, 168-9
Wallace Monument 166
Wars of Independence 148-9
Wars of the Roses 22, 76-7, 131
Webb, Sir Aston 70
Webb, John 84
Westminster Abbey 23, 102, 105
Westminster, Palace of **102-9**, *103, 104, 106, 108*
  House of Commons 102
  House of Lords 102, *104*
  Old Palace Yard 109
  Queen's Robing Room *107*
  St Stephen's Chapel 102, 109
Westminster Hall 105-6, 109
Wet, Jacob de (the Younger) 150
Whitehall Palace 31, 83, 86, 98, 102, 109, 114
William I (the Conqueror) 20, 58, 72, 74, 105, 146
William II (Rufus) 74, 102, 105-6
William III 24, 28, 86, 88, 92, 95, 117, 144
William IV 23, 33, 51, 68, 92, 95, 99
William, Prince 101
William the Lyon 168
William Rufus see William II
Windsor Castle 8, **20-7**, *21, 22, 26-7*, 31, 51, 69, 71, 99
  Royal Lodge 50
  St George's Chapel 20, 22-3, 25, 27
Wolsey, Sir Thomas 28-30, 114
Wren, Sir Christopher 33, 34, 85, 86, 88, 92
Württemberg, Duke of 35
Wyatt, James 25, 50, 91

York House 99
York Place 114

TEXT AND PICTURE CREDITS

Text copyright of Jane Struthers, apart from the entries on Kew Palace (pp.36–9), Leeds Castle (pp.44–5), Somerset House (pp.82–85), Beaumaris (pp.138–9), Dunfermline Abbey and Palace (pp.172–3) and the Castle of Mey (pp.188–9) copyright Scala Quin. All images copyright Chris Coe except for the cover (see jacket for credits) and the following: Bazzarrgh: p.189; Blenheim Palace, reproduced by kind permission of His Grace the Duke of Marlborough: p.122, p.123, p.125 (Chris Andrews); MattBuck4950: p.138; Cadw, by kind permission: p.128, p.129, p.130, p.132, p.133, p.134, p.136; Corbis: p.9, p.47 (Nick Wiseman/Eye Ubiquitous); Istockphoto: p.1 (Anthony Brown), p.45 (Mark Bond); David Iliff: p.26; Leeds Castle Foundation: p.44; Jim Linwood: p.36, p.37; Mary Evans Picture Library: p.83; PA Images: p.188; Nyaa Birdies Perch: p.39; Photolibrary: p.103, p.172, p.173; Lars Ploughmann: p.84; Aashish Rao Photography: p.185; Paul Riddle: p.4, p.16, p.17, p.28, p.32, p.40, p.41, p.42, p.49, p.50, p.63, p.72, p.73, p.74, p.77, p.78, p.80, p.86, p.87, p.89, p.90, p.93, p.114, p.115, p.117, p.118, p.119; The Royal Collection © 2011, Her Majesty Queen Elizabeth II: p.18, p.25 (Mark Fiennes), p.64 (John Freeman), p.65, p.69 (Derry Moore), p.97, p.100 (Jeremy Whitaker), p.154, p.157 (Antonia Reeve); Sandringham Estate, photographs by gracious permission of H.M. The Queen: p.11, p.14; Shutterstock: p.21 (alfredolon), p.53 (ronfromyork), p.82 (Simon Gurney), p.139 (Jarek Janosek), p.160 (Zdenek Krchak); Andy Williams: p.10, p.13, p.46, p.141, p.184, p.186. Every effort has been made to contact copyright holders, but should there by any omissions, New Holland Publishers would be pleased to insert the appropriate acknowledgement in any subsequent printing of this publication.